ROSE HAGE

Edward Hall and Roger Warren

ROSE RAGE

A Propeller Production
adapted from
Shakespeare's *Henry VI* plays

OBERON BOOKS
LONDON

First published in 2001 by Oberon Books Ltd.
(incorporating Absolute Classics)
521 Caledonian Road, London N7 9RH
Tel: 020 7607 3637 / Fax: 020 7607 3629

e-mail: oberon.books@btinternet.com

A catalogue record for this book is available from the British Library.

ISBN: 1 84002 213 2

Cover illustration: Gerald Scarfe

Series design: Richard Doust

Printed in Great Britain by Antony Rowe Ltd, Reading.

ROSE RAGE: THE COMPANY

Edward Hall

Propeller is an all-male Shakespeare company created at the Watermill Theatre in Newbury. Our aim is simple: to perform Shakespeare's plays with a contemporary aesthetic whilst maintaining the necessary emphasis on the spoken word. For us, developing the relationship between the performer and audience in and around the play is of paramount importance. Most of the problems of directing Shakespeare on the modern stage are created by the indoor theatre. The modern director has to deal with electric lights, a stage that bears no architectural resemblance to the theatre of Shakespeare's day, and a two-act tradition with one interval rather than the classical five-act structure. In producing Shakespeare, Propeller attempts to create some of the atmosphere that must have been a large part of the experience of watching plays in the outdoor theatre. To that end, we use live music played and sung by the actors and are constantly looking for new ways, other than scenic, of solving the problems of staging Shakespeare's texts. You may often find that the performance experience begins before you enter the theatre, and continues during the interval, whilst sometimes the action can move in mid-flow from the theatre outside, though not of course in winter...

Rose Rage is our most ambitious project to date, and squeezes three plays into two evenings. I hope in reading this text you will get a strong flavour of Shakespeare's originals, and, if you've seen the productions, something to reflect on about the journey from page to stage.

This company and this text would not exist without the Watermill Theatre. It is vital that the smaller regional producing theatres in this country are financially supported. Grass-roots theatre is the breeding ground for the artists and their work that go on to fill the larger theatres. If we lose many more, our theatre tradition will collapse like a deck of cards, leaving the cultural life of the country substantially poorer.

Edward Hall
Newbury 2001

FROM HENRY VI TO ROSE RAGE: THE ADAPTATION

Roger Warren

When, and even if, Shakespeare wrote the three plays about the reign of King Henry VI attributed to him in the First Folio edition of his works is still the subject of debate; but whether he was wholly or only partly responsible for them, they are likely to be amongst his earliest work, perhaps his very first: 1591–2 seem plausible dates. There is also much argument about whether the three plays were originally designed as a cycle, though that is how they are usually presented in the modern theatre: the narrative is continuous, and several major characters continue from one play to another.

In modern performance the plays are often adapted so that they can be given on two evenings instead of three, as in the Watermill production for which this adaptation was prepared. In addition, Edward Hall's aim was that neither evening should last much longer than two hours. Reducing nine hours of playing time to four obviously involves jettisoning a great deal of the original text: the issue becomes not so much what to omit as what to leave in, and that was determined by the needs of the narrative and by which scenes seemed most crucial dramatically. By omitting completely the Joan of Arc scenes from the original Part One, and those involving the Duchess of Gloucester's witchcraft from the original Part Two, we have been able to condense the Folio's Parts One and Two into our first evening, with the Folio's Part Three occupying our second evening. While our re-shaping involves conflating incidents and even characters, it follows the basic structure of the originals.

Shakespeare's Part One deals with England's loss of France, which had been conquered by Henry VI's father, King Henry V; it is lost because of disunity between the English nobility, and especially because of the quarrel between the Dukes of York and Somerset, vividly dramatised in the fictional episode where they pluck the white and red roses. Their dispute escalates into the Wars of the Roses, which break out at the end of Shakespeare's Part Two and of our first evening. Shakespeare builds Part Two around the destruction of the Lord Protector, Duke Humphrey of Gloucester; the removal of his strong government creates a dangerous political vacuum, providing the opportunity for the rise of the rival claimant for the crown, Richard Duke of York, and his agent Jack Cade, whose popular rebellion anticipates (and parodies) York's aristocratic one. Shakespeare's structure for Part Two provides the shape of our first evening; but we have also attempted to bring the development of the York/Somerset quarrel into sharper focus than in the original, while reinforcing the central importance of the relationship between Henry's queen Margaret and the Duke of Suffolk. When Suffolk is banished for his part in Duke Humphrey's murder and then murdered himself, Margaret's desire for revenge motivates the increasing savagery of her opposition to the house of York and intensifies the violence of the Wars of the Roses, which rage destructively through our second evening; out of this chaos arises the anarchic figure of Richard of Gloucester, the future Richard III.

Despite our extensive cutting and some consequent minor re-writing, our only major addition is the opening speech, the dying words of Henry V from Hall's *Chronicle*, one of Shakespeare's source books. Otherwise the text that remains after cutting follows that of the First Folio closely, and the stage directions are based on those of the Folio. Our text uses lighter punctuation than strictly grammatical modern usage would require, to preserve the shape and rhythm of the lines and to remove unnecessary obstacles to their speaking. The text printed here is the one with which rehearsals began, though further modification was expected to take place during the rehearsal process. We are very grateful to Angie Kendall for helping to prepare it.

Roger Warren
Newbury 2001

Characters

The House of Lancaster

KING HENRY VI

Henry VI's uncles:

DUKE HUMPHREY of Gloucester – the Lord Protector

CARDINAL Beaufort – Bishop of Winchester

Duke of EXETER

Duke of SOMERSET

Earl of SUFFOLK

Sir Humphrey STAFFORD

Lord SAYE

Lord CLIFFORD

YOUNG CLIFFORD – his son

BASSET – supporter of Somerset

Lord TALBOT – general of the English forces in France

JOHN Talbot – his son

MARGARET of Anjou – later Henry VI's Queen

PRINCE EDWARD – her son

The House of York

Richard Plantagenet, Duke of YORK

His sons:

EDWARD – later King Edward IV

GEORGE – later Duke of CLARENCE

RICHARD – later Duke of Gloucester

Edmund, Earl of RUTLAND

York's allies:

Earl of WARWICK

VERNON

A LAWYER

LADY ELIZABETH GREY – later Edward IV's Queen

Lord RIVERS – her brother

The Commons

Jack CADE – leader of the rebellion

Dick the BUTCHER – a rebel

Smith the WEAVER – a rebel

The CLERK of Chatham

A SON that has killed his father

A FATHER that has killed his son

The French

KING LOUIS XI

LADY BONA – his sister

GENERAL of Paris

MESSENGERS

REBELS

SOLDIERS

Rose Rage was first performed at the Watermill Theatre, Newbury, on 3 February 2001, with the following cast:

WARWICK/CADE, Tony Bell

TALBOT/
EDWARD/WEAVER, Dugald Bruce-Lockhart

RICHARD/CLERK/
GENERAL/BASSET, Richard Clothier

EXETER/FIRST REBEL, Emilio Doorgasingh

DUKE HUMPHREY/
YOUNG CLIFFORD/POST/RIVERS, Matt Flynn

MARGARET/
VERNON/MESSENGER, Robert Hands

SUFFOLK/BUTCHER/
GEORGE, (later CLARENCE), Vince Leigh

CARDINAL/SAYE/
PRINCE EDWARD/OLD CLIFFORD, Chris Myles

KING HENRY/
JOHN/LADY BONA, Jonathan McGuinness

SOMERSET/SECOND REBEL/
LADY GREY/RUTLAND/SON, Simon Scardifield

YORK/STAFFORD/
FATHER/KING LOUIS, Guy Williams

Director, Edward Hall

Designer, Michael Pavelka

Lighting, Ben Ormerod

Music devised and arranged by Tony Bell, Vince Leigh and Dugald Bruce-Lockhart

Production Manager, Lawrence T Doyle

Company Stage Manager, Tracey J Cooper

Technical Assistant, Jonathan Thompson

Deputy Stage Manager, Julia Reid

Assistant Stage Manager, Victoria Mowlam

Wardrobe Supervisor, Jonathan Hunt

Scenic Artist, Claire Mallindine

Press and Publicity, Tei Williams

Production Photographer, Laurence Burns

PART ONE

Scene 1

The will of King Henry the Fifth is read:

DUKE HUMPHREY: Since now I shall be taken from you,
I, Henry the Fifth, King of France and England, render
thanks to God that he calls me when I am of perfect
remembrance. This I say:

My brethren and loving friends: if you love me, you
ought to love my child, not for his desert, but for mine.
I charge you all to render your allegiance unto my son,
King Henry the Sixth.

As touching the estate of my realm, I command you to
love and join together in one league and one unfeigned
amity. I will that my brother Humphrey shall be
Protector of England during the minority of my child.
And I command Lord Talbot with fire and sword to
persecute Charles, calling himself Dauphin, to expel
him utterly from our realm of France.

What I have gotten, I charge you keep it; I command
you defend it; and I desire you to nourish it.

*Dead march. Enter the funeral of King Henry the Fifth,
attended on by DUKE HUMPHREY of Gloucester, the Lord
Protector, the Duke of EXETER, CARDINAL Beaufort, and
others.*

DUKE HUMPHREY: Hung be the heavens with black,
                             yield day to night;
Comets importing change of times and states,
Brandish your crystal tresses in the sky,
And with them scourge the bad revolting stars
That have consented unto Henry's death:
King Henry the Fifth, too famous to live long.

What should I say? His deeds exceed all speech.
He ne'er lift up his hand but conquerèd.

CARDINAL: He was a king blest of the King of Kings.
The battles of the Lord of Hosts he fought;
The church's prayers made him so prosperous.

DUKE HUMPHREY: The church? Where is it? Had not
churchmen prayed,
His thread of life had not so soon decayed.
None do you like but an effeminate prince,
Whom like a schoolboy you may overawe.

CARDINAL: Gloucester, whate'er we like, thou art Protector,
And lookest to command the Prince and realm.

EXETER: Cease, cease these jars, and rest your minds in peace.
Henry the Fifth, thy ghost I invocate:
Prosper this realm, keep it from civil broils.
A far more glorious star thy soul will make
Than Julius Caesar or bright –

Enter MESSENGERS.

FIRST MESSENGER: My honourable lords, health to you all.
Sad tidings bring I to you out of France,
Of loss, of slaughter, and discomfiture.
Guyenne, Compiegne, Rouen, Rheims, Orléans,
Bordeaux, Gisors, Poitiers are all quite lost.

EXETER: What sayst thou, man, before dead Henry's corpse?

DUKE HUMPHREY: Is Bordeaux lost? Is Rouen yielded up?

EXETER: How were they lost? What treachery was used?

SECOND MESSENGER: No treachery, but want of men
and money.
Amongst the soldiers this is mutterèd:
That here you maintain several factions,
And whilst a field should be dispatched and fought,
You are disputing of your generals.

FIRST MESSENGER: Awake, awake, English nobility,
    Let not sloth dim your honours new-begot.
    Cropped are the flower-de-luces in your arms;
    Of England's coat, one half is cut away.
    The English army is grown weak and faint,
    And brave Lord Talbot craveth fresh supply.

SECOND MESSENGER: Remember lords, your oaths to
                                        Henry sworn:
    Either to quell the Dauphin utterly,
    Or bring him in obedience to your yoke.

DUKE HUMPHREY: I'll to the Tower with all the haste I can,
    To view th'artillery and munition,
    And then I will proclaim young Henry king. (*Exit.*)

EXETER: To Eltham will I, where the young King is,
    Being ordained his special governor,
    And for his safety there I'll best devise. (*Exit.*)

CARDINAL: Each hath his place and function to attend;
    I am left out, for me nothing remains.
    But long I will not be Jack-out-of-office.
    The King from Eltham I intend to steal,
    And sit at chiefest stern of public weal. (*Exit.*)

Scene 2

A rose garden.

Enter Richard Plantagenet Duke of YORK, the Earl of WARWICK, the Duke of SOMERSET, BASSET, the Earl of SUFFOLK, VERNON, and a LAWYER.

YORK: Great lords and gentlemen, what means this silence?
    Dare no man answer in a case of truth?

SUFFOLK: Within the Temple hall we were too loud.
    The garden here is more convenient.

YORK: Then Suffolk, say if I maintained the truth;
 Or else was wrangling Somerset in th'error?

SUFFOLK: Faith, I have been a truant in the law,
 And never yet could frame my will to it,
 And therefore frame the law unto my will.

SOMERSET: Judge you, my lord of Warwick, then between us.

WARWICK: In all these nice sharp quillets of the law,
 Good faith, I am no wiser than a daw.

YORK: Since you are tongue-tied and so loath to speak,
 In dumb significants proclaim your thoughts.
 Let him that is a true-born gentleman,
 If he suppose that I have pleaded truth,
 From off this briar pluck a white rose with me.

He plucks a white rose.

SOMERSET: Let him that is no coward nor no flatterer,
 But dare maintain the party of the truth,
 Pluck a red rose from off this thorn with me.

He plucks a red rose.

WARWICK: I love no colours, and without all colour
 Of base insinuating flattery
 I pluck this white rose with Plantagenet.

SUFFOLK: I pluck this red rose with young Somerset,
 And say withal I think he held the right.

VERNON: Stay, lords and gentlemen, and pluck no more
 Till you conclude that he upon whose side
 The fewest roses are cropped from the tree
 Shall yield the other in the right opinion.

SOMERSET: Good Master Vernon, it is well objected.
 If I have fewest, I subscribe in silence.

YORK: And I.

VERNON: Then for the truth and plainness of the case
 I pluck this pale and maiden blossom here,
 Giving my verdict on the white rose side.

SOMERSET: Prick not your finger as you pluck it off,
 Lest bleeding, you do paint the white rose red,
 And fall on my side so against your will.

LAWYER: Unless my study and my books be false,
 The argument you held was wrong in law,
 In sign whereof I pluck a white rose too.

YORK: Now Somerset, where is your argument?

SOMERSET: Here in my scabbard, meditating that
 Shall dye your white rose in a bloody red.

YORK: Meantime your cheeks do counterfeit our roses,
 For pale they look with fear, as witnessing
 The truth on our side.

SOMERSET: No, Plantagenet,
 'Tis not for fear, but anger, that thy cheeks
 Blush for pure shame to counterfeit our roses,
 And yet thy tongue will not confess thy error.

YORK: Hath not thy rose a canker, Somerset?

SOMERSET: Hath not thy rose a thorn, Plantagenet?

YORK: Ay, sharp and piercing, to maintain his truth.

SOMERSET: Well, I'll find friends to wear my bleeding roses,
 That shall maintain what I have said is true.

YORK: Now by this maiden blossom in my hand,
 I scorn thee and thy faction, peevish boy.

SOMERSET: Away, away,
 We grace the yeoman by conversing with him.

WARWICK: Now by God's will, thou wrong'st him, Somerset.
 His grandfather was Lionel Duke of Clarence,

    Third son to the third Edward, King of England.
    Spring crestless yeomen from so deep a root?

SOMERSET: Was not thy father, Richard Duke of York,
    For treason executed in our late king's days,
    And by his treason stand'st not thou attainted?

YORK: My father was attachèd, not attainted,
    Condemned to die for treason, but no traitor;
    And that I'll prove on better men than Somerset,
    Look to it well, and say you are well warned.

SOMERSET: Ah, thou shalt find us ready for thee still,
    And know us by these colours for thy foes,
    For these, my friends in spite of thee shall wear.

YORK: And by my soul, this pale and angry rose,
    As cognizance of my blood-drinking hate,
    Will I forever and my faction wear
    Until it wither with me to my grave,
    Or flourish to the height of my degree.

SUFFOLK: Go forward and be choked with thy ambition.
    And so farewell until I meet thee next. (*Exit.*)

SOMERSET: Have with thee, Suffolk. Farewell, ambitious
                         York. (*Exit.*)

YORK: How am I braved, and must perforce endure it!
    Now give me leave to satisfy myself
    In craving your opinion of my title,
    Which is infallible, to England's crown.

WARWICK: Sweet York begin, and if thy claim be good
    Then Warwick is thy subject to command.

YORK: I claim the crown by birth and parentage:
    For by my mother I derivèd am
    From Lionel Duke of Clarence, the third son
    To King Edward the Third, while Henry
    From John of Gaunt doth trace his pedigree,
    Being but fourth of that heroic line.

So, if the issue of the elder son
Succeed before the younger, I am King.

WARWICK: What plain proceedings is more plain than this?
Henry doth claim the crown from John of Gaunt,
The fourth son, York claims it from the third.
And so, in signal of my love to thee,
Will I upon thy party wear this rose.
My heart assures me that the Earl of Warwick
Shall one day make the Duke of York a king.

YORK: And Warwick, this I do assure myself:
Richard shall live to make the Earl of Warwick
The greatest man in England but the King.

WARWICK: And here I prophesy: this brawl today,
Grown to this faction in the Temple garden,
Shall send between the red rose and the white,
A thousand souls to death and deadly night.

YORK: Come, let us in to dinner. I dare say
This quarrel will drink blood another day.

Exeunt.

BASSET: (*Detaining VERNON.*) Stay, sir.
Dar'st thou maintain the former words thou spak'st
Against my lord the Duke of Somerset?

VERNON: Sirrah, thy lord I honour as he is.

BASSET: Why, what is he? As good a man as York.

VERNON: Hark ye, not so; in witness take ye that. (*Strikes him.*)

BASSET: Villain, I'll to his majesty and crave
I may have liberty to venge this wrong,
When thou shalt see I'll meet thee to thy cost.

VERNON: Well miscreant, I'll be there as soon as you,
And after meet you, sooner than you would.

Exeunt.

Scene 3

Parliament.

Flourish. Enter KING HENRY, EXETER, DUKE HUMPHREY, CARDINAL; SOMERSET and the Earl of SUFFOLK with red roses; WARWICK and YORK with white roses.

DUKE HUMPHREY offers to put up a bill; the CARDINAL snatches it, tears it.

CARDINAL: Com'st thou with deep premeditated lines,
With written pamphlets studiously devised?
Humphrey of Gloucester, if thou canst accuse,
Or aught intend'st to lay unto my charge,
Do it without invention suddenly,
As I with sudden and extemporal speech
Purpose to answer what thou canst object.

DUKE HUMPHREY: Presumptuous priest, this place
commands my patience,
Or thou shouldst find thou hast dishonoured me.

CARDINAL: Gloucester, you think no-one should sway but you,
No one but you should be about the King;
But you shall know I am as good –

DUKE HUMPHREY: As good?
Thou bastard of my grandfather.

CARDINAL: Ay lordly sir, for what are you, I pray,
But one imperious in another's throne?

DUKE HUMPHREY: Am I not Protector, saucy priest?

CARDINAL: Unreverent Gloucester.

DUKE HUMPHREY: Thou art reverent
Touching thy spiritual function, not thy life.

CARDINAL: Rome shall remedy this.

DUKE HUMPHREY: Roam thither then.

KING HENRY: Uncles of Gloucester and of Winchester,
    The special watchmen of our English weal,
    I would prevail, if prayers might prevail,
    To join your hearts in love and amity.
    O what a scandal is it to our crown
    That two such noble peers as ye should jar!
    Believe me, lords, my tender years can tell
    Civil dissension is a viperous worm
    That gnaws the bowels of the commonwealth.

WARWICK: Yield, my lord Protector; yield, Winchester.

CARDINAL: He shall submit, or I will never yield.

DUKE HUMPHREY: Compassion on the King commands
                                        me stoop.

WARWICK: Behold, my lord of Winchester, the Duke
    Hath banished moody discontented fury.
    Why look you still so stern and tragical?

DUKE HUMPHREY: Here Winchester, I offer thee my hand.

KING HENRY: Fie Uncle Beaufort, I have heard you preach
    That malice was a great and grievous sin;
    And will not you maintain the thing you teach?

WARWICK: For shame, my lord of Winchester, relent.
    What, shall a child instruct you what to do?

CARDINAL: Well, Duke of Gloucester, I will yield to thee.
    Love for thy love, and hand for hand I give.

DUKE HUMPHREY: (*Aside.*) Ay, but I fear me with a
                                        hollow heart.
    (*To the others.*) So help me God, as I dissemble not.

CARDINAL: (*Aside.*) So help me God as I intend it not.

KING HENRY: O loving uncle, kind Duke of Gloucester,
    How joyful am I made by this contract!

*Enter VERNON wearing a white rose, and BASSET wearing
a red rose.*

VERNON: Grant me the combat, gracious sovereign.

BASSET: And me, my lord, grant me the combat, too.

YORK: This is my servant; hear him, noble Prince.

SOMERSET: And this is mine, sweet Henry, favour him.

KING HENRY: Be patient, lords, and give them leave to speak.

BASSET: This fellow here with envious carping tongue
    Upbraided me about the rose I wear,
    Saying the sanguine colour of the leaves
    Did represent my master's blushing cheeks,
    In confutation of which rude reproach,
    And in defence of my lord's worthiness,
    I crave the benefit of law of arms.

VERNON: And that is my petition, noble lord;
    For he first took exceptions at this badge,
    Pronouncing that the paleness of this flower
    Bewrayed the faintness of my master's heart.

YORK: Will not this malice, Somerset, be left?

SOMERSET: Your private grudge, my lord of York, will out,
    Though ne'er so cunningly you smother it.

KING: Good Lord, what madness rules in brainsick men
    When for so slight and frivolous a cause
    Such factious emulations shall arise?
    Good cousins both of York and Somerset,
    Quiet yourselves, I pray, and be at peace.

YORK: Let this dissension first be tried by fight,
    And then your highness shall command a peace.

SOMERSET: The quarrel toucheth none but us alone;
    Betwixt ourselves let us decide it then.

DUKE HUMPHREY: Presumptuous vassals, are you not
ashamed

With this immodest clamorous outrage
To trouble and disturb the King and us?
And you, my lords, methinks you do not well
To bear with their perverse objections,
Much less to take occasion from their mouths
To raise a mutiny betwixt yourselves.
Let me persuade you take a better course.

EXETER: It grieves his highness. Good my lords, be friends.

KING HENRY: Let me be umpire in this doubtful strife.
I see no reason, if I wear this rose,

He takes a red rose.

That anyone should therefore be suspicious
I more incline to Somerset than York.
Both are my kinsmen, and I love them both.
Cousin of York, we institute your grace
To be our regent in our realm of France;
And good my lord of Somerset, unite
Your troops of horsemen with his bands of foot.
Go cheerfully together and digest
Your angry choler on our enemies.

Exeunt all but EXETER.

EXETER: Ay, we may march in England or in France
Not seeing what is likely to ensue:
This late dissension grown betwixt the peers
Burns under feignèd ashes of forged love,
And will at last break out into a flame.
And now I fear that fatal prophecy
Which in the time of Henry the Fifth,
Was in the mouth of every sucking babe:
That Henry born at Monmouth should win all,
And Henry born at Windsor should lose all:

Which is so plain that Exeter doth wish
His days may finish ere that hapless time. (*Exit.*)

Scene 4

Enter Lord TALBOT and his army before the walls of Paris.

TALBOT: Go to the gates of Paris, trumpeter.
Summon their general unto the wall.

The trumpeter sounds a parley. Enter French GENERAL, aloft.

English John Talbot, captain, calls you forth,
Servant in arms to Harry King of England,
And thus he would: open your city gates,
Be humble to us, call my sovereign yours
And do him homage as obedient subjects,
And I'll withdraw me and my bloody power.
But if you frown upon this proffered peace,
You tempt the fury of my three attendants,
Lean famine, quartering steel, and climbing fire,
Who in a moment even with the earth
Shall lay your stately and air-braving towers
If you forsake the offer of their love.

GENERAL: Thou ominous and fearful owl of death,
Our nation's terror and their bloody scourge,
The period of thy tyranny approacheth.
On either hand thee there are squadrons pitched
To wall thee from the liberty of flight,
And no way canst thou turn thee for redress
But death doth front thee with apparent spoil,
And pale destruction meets thee in the face.

Drum afar off.

Hark, hark, the Dauphin's drum, a warning bell,
Sings heavy music to thy timorous soul,
And mine shall ring thy dire departure out. (*Exit.*)

TALBOT: He fables not, I hear the enemy.
    O negligent and heedless discipline,
    How are we parked and bounded in a pale:
    A little herd of England's timorous deer
    Mazed with a yelping kennel of French curs.
    Sell every man his life as dear as mine
    And they shall find dear deer of us, my friends.
    God and Saint George, Talbot and England's right,
    Prosper our colours in this dangerous fight!

The battle begins as TALBOT is ambushed.

Meanwhile in another part of France…

Enter YORK and many SOLDIERS.

YORK: A plague upon that villain Somerset
    That thus delays my promisèd supply
    Of horsemen that were levied for this siege!
    Renownèd Talbot doth expect my aid,
    And I am louted by a traitor villain
    And cannot help the noble chevalier.
    God comfort him in this necessity;
    If he miscarry, farewell wars in France!

Enter EXETER.

EXETER: Thou princely leader of our English strength,
    Spur to the rescue of the noble Talbot,
    Who now is girdled with a waste of iron
    And hemmed about with grim destruction.

YORK: O God, that Somerset, who in proud heart
    Denies my horsemen, were in Talbot's place!
    So should we save a valiant gentleman
    By forfeiting a traitor and a coward.

EXETER: O send some succour to the distressed lord.

YORK: He dies, we lose; I break my warlike word;
    We mourn, France smiles; we lose, they daily get,
    All 'long of this vile traitor Somerset.

EXETER: Then God take mercy on brave Talbot's soul,
  And on his son young John, who two hours since
  I met in travel toward his warlike father.
  This seven years did not Talbot see his son,
  And now they meet where both their lives are done.

YORK: Exeter, farewell. No more my fortune can
  But curse the cause I cannot aid the man.
  Maine, Blois, Poitiers, and Tours are won away
  'Long all of Somerset and his delay.

Exeunt all but EXETER.

EXETER: Thus while the vulture of sedition
  Feeds in the bosom of such great commanders,
  Sleeping neglection doth betray to loss
  The conquest of our scarce-cold conqueror,
  That ever-living man of memory,
  Henry the Fifth. Whiles they each other cross,
  Lives, honours, lands, and all hurry to loss. (*Exit.*)

Back at Paris...

Enter TALBOT and his son JOHN. They are surrounded.

TALBOT: O young John Talbot, I did send for thee
  To tutor thee in stratagems of war,
  Now thou art come unto a feast of death.
  Therefore dear boy, mount on my swiftest horse,
  And I'll direct thee how thou shalt escape
  By sudden flight. Come, dally not, be gone.

JOHN: Is my name Talbot, and am I your son,
  And shall I fly? Dishonour not my mother.
  The world will say he is not Talbot's blood
  That basely fled when noble Talbot stood.

TALBOT: Fly to revenge my death if I be slain.

JOHN: He that flies so will ne'er return again.
  Stay, go, do what you will; the like do I,
  For live I will not if my father die.

TALBOT: Then here I take my leave of thee, fair son,
    Born to eclipse thy life this afternoon.

Alarum.

In another part of France…

*Enter SOMERSET and SUFFOLK with an army. They
meet EXETER.*

SOMERSET: How now, Lord Exeter, whither were you sent?

EXETER: Whither, my lord? From bought and sold Lord
                                        Talbot,
    Who ringed about with bold adversity,
    Cries out for help from York and Somerset.

SOMERSET: It is too late, I cannot help him now.

SUFFOLK: This expedition was by York and Talbot
    Too rashly plotted. The over-daring Talbot
    Hath sullied all his gloss of former honour
    By this unheedful, desperate, wild adventure.

SOMERSET: York set him on to fight and die in shame,
    That Talbot dead, great York might bear the name.

EXETER: Let not your private discord keep away
    The levied succours that should lend him aid.

SOMERSET: York set him on, York should have sent him aid.

EXETER: And York as fast upon your grace exclaims,
    Swearing that you withhold his levied horse
    Collected for this expedition.

SOMERSET: York lies. He might have sent and had the horse.
    I owe him little duty and less love,
    And take foul scorn to fawn on him by sending.

EXETER: The fraud of England, not the force of France,
    Hath now entrapped the noble-minded Talbot.

Never to England shall he bear his life,
But dies betrayed to fortune by your strife.

SOMERSET: Come, go. I will dispatch the horsemen
straight.

Within six hours they will be at his aid.

EXETER: Too late comes rescue, he is ta'en or slain.

SOMERSET: If he be dead, brave Talbot, then adieu.

EXETER: His fame lives in the world, his shame in you.

Exeunt severally.

Alarum. Enter TALBOT's son, fighting. He is mortally wounded.

Enter TALBOT fighting.

TALBOT: Saint George and victory! Fight, soldiers, fight!
The Regent hath with Talbot broke his word,
And left us to the rage of France's sword.

He is mortally wounded.

Where is my other life? Mine own is gone.
Dizzy-eyed fury and great rage of heart
Suddenly made him from my side to start
Into the clust'ring battle of the French,
And in that sea of blood my boy did drench
His over-mounting spirit; and there died
My Icarus, my blossom, in his pride.
O where's young Talbot, where is valiant John?

He sees his dying son.

Triumphant death smeared with captivity,
Young Talbot's valour makes me smile at thee.
O thou whose wounds become hard-favoured death,
Speak to thy father ere thou yield thy breath.
My spirit can no longer bear these harms.

Soldiers, adieu. I have what I would have,
Now my old arms are young John Talbot's grave. (*He dies.*)

Scene 5

The plains of Anjou.

Alarum. Enter SUFFOLK with MARGARET in his hand.

SUFFOLK: Be what thou wilt, thou art my prisoner.

He gazes on her.

O fairest beauty, do not fear nor fly,
For I will touch thee but with reverent hands.
Who art thou, say, that I may honour thee.

MARGARET: Margaret my name, and daughter to a king,
The King of Naples, whosoe'er thou art.

SUFFOLK: An earl I am, and Suffolk am I called.
Be not offended, nature's miracle,
Thou art allotted to be ta'en by me.
Yet if this servile usage once offend,
Go, and be free again, as Suffolk's friend.

She is going.

O stay! (*Aside.*) I have no power to let her pass.
My hand would free her, but my heart says no.

MARGARET: Say Earl of Suffolk, if thy name be so,
What ransom must I pay before I pass?
For I perceive I am thy prisoner.

SUFFOLK: (*Aside.*) She's beautiful, and therefore to be wooed;
She is a woman, therefore to be won.

MARGARET: Wilt thou accept of ransom, yea or no?

SUFFOLK: (*Aside.*) Fond man, remember that thou hast a wife;
Then how can Margaret be thy paramour?

MARGARET: (*Aside.*) He talks at random; sure the man is mad.

SUFFOLK: (*Aside.*) I'll win this Lady Margaret. For whom?
    Why, for my king – tush, that's a wooden thing.

MARGARET: (*Aside.*) He talks of wood: it is some carpenter.

SUFFOLK: Madam, I have a secret to reveal.

MARGARET: (*Aside.*) What though I be enthralled, he
                                        seems a knight,
    And will not any way dishonour me.

SUFFOLK: Lady, vouchsafe to listen what I say.

MARGARET: (*Aside.*) Perhaps I shall be rescued by the French,
    And then I need not crave his courtesy.

SUFFOLK: Sweet madam, give me hearing in a cause.

MARGARET: (*Aside.*) Tush, women have been captivate ere
                                                now.

SUFFOLK: Lady, wherefore talk you so?

MARGARET: I cry you mercy, 'tis but *quid* for *quo*.

SUFFOLK: Say, gentle Princess, would you not suppose
    Your bondage happy to be made a queen?

MARGARET: To be a queen in bondage is more vile
    Than is a slave in base servility,
    For princes should be free.

SUFFOLK: And so shall you.
    I'll undertake to make thee Henry's queen,
    To put a golden sceptre in thy hand,
    And set a precious crown upon thy head,
    If thou wilt condescend to be my –

MARGARET: What?

SUFFOLK: His love.

MARGARET: I am unworthy to be Henry's wife.

SUFFOLK: No, gentle madam, I unworthy am
    To woo so fair a dame to be his wife.
    How say you, madam, are ye so content?

MARGARET: An if my father please, I am content.

SUFFOLK: I'll crave a parley to confer with him.
    Farewell, sweet madam; but hark you, Margaret,
    No princely commendations to my king?

MARGARET: Such commendations as becomes a maid,
    A virgin, and his servant, say to him.

She is going.

SUFFOLK: But madam, I must trouble you again –
    No loving token to his majesty?

MARGARET: Yes, my good lord: a pure unspotted heart,
    Never yet taint with love, I send the King.

SUFFOLK: And this withal.

He kisses her.

MARGARET: That for thyself; I will not so presume
    To send such peevish tokens to a king. (*Exit.*)

SUFFOLK: O wert thou for myself! – but Suffolk, stay,
    Thou mayst not wander in that labyrinth.
    There Minotaurs and ugly treasons lurk.
    Solicit Henry with her wondrous praise
    That may bereave him of his wits with wonder.
    For so my fancy may be satisfied,
    And peace establishèd between these realms.
    Margaret shall now be queen, and rule the King,
    But I will rule both her, the King, and realm. (*Exit.*)

Scene 6

Sennet. Enter KING HENRY and DUKE HUMPHREY with letters.

KING HENRY: Have you perused the letters from the Pope?

DUKE HUMPHREY: I have my lord, and their intent is this:
    They humbly sue unto your excellence
    To have a godly peace concluded of
    Between the realms of England and of France.

KING HENRY: How doth your grace affect their motion?

DUKE HUMPHREY: Well, my good lord, and as the only means
    To stop effusion of our Christian blood.

KING HENRY: Ay marry, uncle, for I always thought
    It was both impious and unnatural
    That such immanity and bloody strife
    Should reign among professors of one faith.

Enter SUFFOLK.

Your wondrous rare description, noble Earl, (*Indicating letters.*)
Of beauteous Margaret hath astonished me.

SUFFOLK: And which is more, she is not so divine,
    So full replete with choice of all delights,
    But with as humble lowliness of mind
    She is content to be at your command –
    Command, I mean, of virtuous chaste intents,
    To love and honour Henry as her lord.

HENRY: And otherwise will Henry ne'er presume.
    Therefore my lord Protector, give consent
    That Marg'ret may be England's royal queen.

DUKE HUMPHREY: So should I give consent to flatter sin.
    You know, my lord, your highness is betrothed
    Unto another lady of esteem.

How shall we then dispense with that contract
And not deface your honour with reproach?

SUFFOLK: As doth a ruler with unlawful oaths
Which therefore may be broke without offence.
A poor earl's daughter is unequal odds.

DUKE HUMPHREY: Why what, I pray, is Margaret more
than that?

SUFFOLK: O yes, my lord, her father is a king,
The King of Naples and Jerusalem,
And of such great authority in France
As his alliance will confirm our peace
And keep the Frenchmen in allegiance.

KING HENRY: Then yield, my lord, and here conclude
with me
That Margaret shall be England's royal queen.
Go Suffolk, bring her to our presence straight;
And you, good uncle, banish all offence.

*Flourish. SUFFOLK leads on MARGARET, attended by
YORK, CARDINAL, WARWICK, and SOMERSET.*

SUFFOLK: Before your high imperial majesty
I humbly now upon my bended knee,
In sight of England and her lordly peers,
Deliver up the Lady Margaret:
The happiest gift that ever marquis gave,
The fairest queen that ever king received.

KING HENRY: Suffolk, arise. Welcome Queen Margaret.
I can express no kinder sign of love
Than this kind kiss. O Lord that lends me life,
Lend me a heart replete with thankfulness!
For thou hast given me in this beauteous face
A world of earthly blessings to my soul,
If sympathy of love unite our thoughts.

MARGARET: Great King of England, and my gracious lord,
    The mutual conference that my mind hath had –
    By day, by night; waking, and in my dreams;
    In courtly company, or at my beads –
    With you, mine alderliefest sovereign,
    Makes me the bolder to salute my king
    With ruder terms, such as my wit affords,
    And overjoy of heart doth minister.

KING HENRY: Her sight did ravish, but her grace in speech,
    Makes me from wond'ring fall to weeping joys,
    Such is the fullness of my heart's content.
    Lords, with one cheerful voice, welcome my love.

LORDS: (*Kneeling.*) Long live Queen Margaret, England's
                                    happiness.

MARGARET: We thank you all.

Flourish. They all rise.

SUFFOLK: My Lord Protector, so it please your grace,
    Here are the articles of contracted peace
    Between our sovereign and the French King Charles,
    For eighteen months concluded by consent.

DUKE HUMPHREY: (*Reads.*) 'Imprimis: it is agreed
                            between the
    French King Charles and William de la Pole, Marquis
    of Suffolk, ambassador for Henry, King of England, that
    the said Henry shall espouse the Lady Margaret,
    daughter unto René, King of Naples, Sicilia, and
    Jerusalem, and crown her Queen of England.
    Item: that the duchy of Anjou and the county of
    Maine shall be released and delivered to the
    King her fa –'

He lets the paper fall.

KING HENRY: Uncle, how now?

DUKE HUMPHREY: Pardon me, gracious lord.
 Some sudden qualm hath struck me at the heart
 And dimmed mine eyes that I can read no further.

KING HENRY: (*To CARDINAL.*) Uncle of Winchester, I pray
 read on.

CARDINAL: (*Reads.*) 'Item: it is further agreed
 between them that the duchies of Anjou and Maine
 shall be released and delivered to the King her
 father, and she sent over of the King of England's
 own proper cost and charges, without having any dowry.'

KING HENRY: They please us well. Lord Marquis, kneel
 down.

 We here create thee the first Duke of Suffolk,
 And gird thee with the sword. Cousin of York,
 We here discharge your grace from being regent
 I'th' parts of France till term of eighteen months
 Be full expired. My lords, we thank you all
 For entertainment to my princely Queen.
 Come, let us in, and with all speed provide
 To see her coronation be performed.

 *Flourish. Exeunt KING HENRY, Queen MARGARET, and
 SUFFOLK. DUKE HUMPHREY stays all the rest.*

DUKE HUMPHREY: Brave peers of England, pillars of
 the state,
 To you Duke Humphrey must unload his grief,
 Your grief, the common grief of all the land.
 What, did my brother Henry spend his youth,
 His valour, coin, and people in the wars,
 To conquer France, his true inheritance?
 Have you yourselves, Somerset, York, and Warwick,
 Received deep scars in France and Normandy,
 To keep by strategy what Henry got?
 Or hath mine uncle Beaufort and myself,
 With all the learnèd Council of the realm,
 Studied so long, debating to and fro,

35

How France and Frenchmen might be kept in awe,
And shall these labours and these honours die?
O peers of England, shameful is this league,
Fatal this marriage, cancelling your fame,
Undoing all, as all had never been!

YORK: For Suffolk's Duke, may he be suffocate
That dims the honour of this warlike isle.
Is all our travail turned to this effect?
After the slaughter of so many men
That sold their bodies for their country's benefit,
Shall we at last conclude effeminate peace?
O Warwick, Warwick, I foresee with grief
The utter loss of all the realm of France.

WARWICK: I never read but England's kings have had
Large sums of gold and dowries with their wives,
And our King Henry gives away his own,
To match with her that brings no vantages.

DUKE HUMPHREY: She should have stayed in France
and starved in France

Before –

CARDINAL: My lord of Gloucester, now ye grow too hot!
It was the pleasure of my lord the King.

DUKE HUMPHREY: My lord of Winchester, I know your
mind.

'Tis not my speeches that you do mislike,
But 'tis my presence that doth trouble ye.
Rancour will out, proud prelate, in thy face
I see thy fury. If I longer stay
We shall begin our ancient bickerings.
Lordings, farewell, and say when I am gone,
I prophesied France will be lost ere long. (*Exit.*)

CARDINAL: So, there goes our Protector in a rage.
'Tis known to you he is mine enemy;
Nay more, an enemy unto you all,

And no great friend, I fear me, to the King.
Consider, lords, he is the next of blood
And heir apparent to the English crown.
What though the common people favour him,
Calling him 'Humphrey, the good Duke of Gloucester',
I fear me, lords, for all this flattering gloss,
He will be found a dangerous Protector.

SOMERSET: Why should he then protect our sovereign,
He being of age to govern of himself?

CARDINAL: Cousin of Somerset, join you with me,
And all together, with the Duke of Suffolk,
We'll quickly hoist Duke Humphrey from his seat.

SOMERSET: This weighty business will not brook delay.

CARDINAL: Let's to the Duke of Suffolk presently.

Exeunt CARDINAL and SOMERSET.

WARWICK: Cousin of York, though Humphrey's pride
And greatness of his place be grief to us,
Yet let us watch the haughty Cardinal;
If Gloucester be displaced, he'll be Protector.

YORK: Or thou or I will be Protector, Warwick,
Despite Duke Humphrey or the Cardinal.
Do you as I do in these dangerous days,
Wink at the Duke of Suffolk's insolence,
At Beaufort's pride, at Somerset's ambition,
Till they have snared the shepherd of the flock,
That virtuous prince, the good Duke Humphrey.
'Tis that they seek, and they, in seeking that,
Shall find their deaths, if York can prophesy.

WARWICK: My lord, break off; I know your mind at full.
(*Exit.*)

YORK: Anjou and Maine are given to the French,
Paris is lost, the state of Normandy

37

Stands on a tickle point now they are gone;
Cold news for me, for I had hope of France,
Even as I have of fertile England's soil.
Suffolk concluded on the articles,
The peers agreed, and Henry was well pleased
To change two dukedoms for a duke's fair daughter.
I cannot blame them all, what is't to them?
'Tis mine they give away and not their own.
A day will come when I shall claim the crown,
For that's the golden mark I seek to hit.
Nor shall proud Lancaster usurp my right,
Nor hold the sceptre in his childish fist,
Nor wear the diadem upon his head
Whose church-like humours fits not for a crown.
Then York, be still a while till time do serve.
Watch thou and wake when others be asleep,
To pry into the secrets of the state,
Till Henry surfeit in the joys of love
With his new bride and England's dear-bought queen,
And Humphrey with the peers be fall'n at jars.
Then will I raise aloft the milk-white rose,
With whose sweet smell the air shall be perfumed,
And in my standard bear the arms of York,
To grapple with the house of Lancaster;
And force perforce I'll make him yield the crown,
Whose bookish rule hath pulled fair England down. (*Exit.*)

Scene 7

Enter SUFFOLK and MARGARET.

MARGARET: My lord of Suffolk, say, is this the guise?
Is this the government of Britain's isle?
What, shall King Henry be a pupil still
Under the surly Gloucester's governance?
Am I a queen in title and in style,
And must be made a subject to a duke?

I thought King Henry had resembled thee
In courage, courtship, and proportion;
But all his mind is bent to holiness,
To number Ave-Maries on his beads.
His champions are the prophets and apostles,
His weapons holy saws of sacred writ,
His study is his tilt-yard, and his loves
Are brazen images of canonized saints.
I would the college of the cardinals
Would choose him Pope, and carry him to Rome,
And set the triple crown upon his head;
That were a state fit for his holiness.

SUFFOLK: Madam, be patient; as I was cause
 Your highness came to England, so will I
 In England work your grace's full content.

MARGARET: Beside the haughty Protector have we Beaufort
 The imperious churchman, Somerset, Warwick,
 And grumbling York; and not the least of these
 But can do more in England than the King.

SUFFOLK: But madam, list to me,
 Although we fancy not the Cardinal,
 Yet must we join with him and with the lords
 Till we have brought Duke Humphrey in disgrace.
 Then one by one we'll weed them all at last,
 And you yourself shall steer the happy helm.

*Sound a sennet. Enter KING HENRY with YORK and
SOMERSET on either side of him whispering with him.*

Also enter DUKE HUMPHREY, WARWICK, and CARDINAL.

KING HENRY: For my part, noble lords, I care not which:
 Or Somerset or York, all's one to me.

YORK: If York have ill demeaned himself in France
 Then let him be denied the regentship.

SOMERSET: If Somerset be unworthy of the place,
Let York be regent, I will yield to him.

WARWICK: Whether your grace be worthy, yea or no,
Dispute not that: York is the worthier.

CARDINAL: Ambitious Warwick, let thy betters speak.

WARWICK: The Cardinal's not my better in the field.

CARDINAL: All in this presence are thy betters, Warwick.

DUKE HUMPHREY: Peace uncle, and show some reason
to us all,
Why Somerset should be preferred in this.

MARGARET: Because the King, forsooth, will have it so.

DUKE HUMPHREY: Madam, the King is old enough himself
To give his censure. These are no women's matters.

MARGARET: If he be old enough, what needs your grace
To be Protector of his excellence?

DUKE HUMPHREY: Madam, I am Protector of the realm,
And at his pleasure will resign my place.

SUFFOLK: Resign it then, and leave thine insolence.
Since thou wert king – as who is king but thou? –
The commonwealth hath daily run to wrack.

CARDINAL: The commons hast thou racked, the clergy's bags
Are lank and lean with thy extortions.

SOMERSET: Thy sumptuous buildings and thy wife's attire
Have cost a mass of public treasury.

MARGARET: Thy sale of offices and towns in France –
If they were known, as the suspect is great –
Would make thee quickly hop without thy head.

DUKE HUMPHREY: As for your spiteful false objections,
Prove them, and I lie open to the law.
But God in mercy so deal with my soul

As I in duty love my King and country.
But to the matter that we have in hand:
I say, my sovereign, York is meetest man
To be your regent in the realm of France.

SUFFOLK: Before we make election, give me leave
To show some reason of no little force
That York is most unmeet of any man.

YORK: I'll tell thee, Suffolk, why I am unmeet:
First, for I cannot flatter thee in pride;
Next, if I be appointed for the place,
My lord of Somerset will keep me here
Without discharge, money, or furniture,
Till France be won into the Dauphin's hands.
Last time I danced attendance on his will
Till Paris was besieged, famished, and lost.

WARWICK: That can I witness, and a fouler fact
Did never traitor in the land commit.

SUFFOLK: Peace, headstrong Warwick.

WARWICK: Image of pride, why should I hold my peace?

YORK: Why, Suffolk, England knows thine insolence.

MARGARET: And thy ambition, York.

KING HENRY: I prithee peace,
Good Queen, and whet not on these furious peers,
For blessed are the peacemakers on earth.
Good uncle, what shall we say to this?

DUKE HUMPHREY: My lords, accept Duke Humphrey's
doom –

Enter BASSET hastily.

BASSET: A sort of naughty persons, lewdly bent,
Under the countenance and confederacy
Of Lady Eleanor, the Protector's wife,

41

The ringleader and head of all this rout,
Have practised dangerously against your state,
Dealing with witches and with conjurors,
Whom we have apprehended in the fact,
Raising up wicked spirits from under ground,
Demanding of King Henry's life and death,
And other of your highness' Privy Council,
As more at large your grace shall understand.

KING HENRY: O God, what mischiefs work the wicked ones,
Heaping confusion on their own heads thereby.

MARGARET: Gloucester, see here the tainture of thy nest,
And look thyself be faultless, thou wert best.

DUKE HUMPHREY: Madam, for myself, to heaven I do
appeal,
How I have loved my King and common weal;
But for my wife, I know not how it stands.
Sorry I am to hear what I have heard.
Noble she is, but if she have forgot
Honour and virtue and conversed with such
As like to pitch, defile nobility,
I banish her my bed and company,
And give her as a prey to law and shame
That hath dishonoured Gloucester's honest name.
I do beseech your majesty give me leave to go.

KING HENRY: Stay, Humphrey Duke of Gloucester, ere
thou go,
Give up thy staff. Henry will to himself
Protector be; and God shall be my hope,
My stay, my guide, and lantern to my feet.
And go in peace, Humphrey, no less beloved
Than when thou wert Protector to thy King.

MARGARET: Give up your staff, sir, and the King his realm.

DUKE HUMPHREY: My staff? Here, noble Henry, is my
staff.

42

As willingly do I the same resign
As erst thy father Henry made it mine;
And even as willing at thy feet I leave it
As others would ambitiously receive it.
Farewell, good King. When I am dead and gone,
May honourable peace attend thy throne. (*Exit.*)

MARGARET: Why, now is Henry King and Margaret Queen,
And Humphrey Duke of Gloucester scarce himself.
Let's look into this business thoroughly,
And call these foul offenders to their answers.

KING HENRY: Go, fetch our uncle back to answer this.

Exit SOMERSET.

Let's poise the cause in justice equal scales,
Whose beam stands sure, whose rightful cause prevails.

MARGARET: Can you not see, or will ye not observe,
How insolent of late he is become,
Disdaining duty that to us belongs?
Small curs are not regarded when they grin,
But great men tremble when the lion roars,
And Humphrey is no little man in England.
First note that he is near you in descent,
And should you fall, he is the next will mount.
By flattery hath he won the commons' hearts,
And when he please to make commotion,
'Tis to be feared they all will follow him.
Now 'tis the spring, and weeds are shallow-rooted;
Suffer them now, and they'll o'ergrow the garden,
And choke the herbs for want of husbandry.
My lords of Suffolk, Winchester, and York,
Reprove my allegation if you can,
Or else conclude my words effectual.

SUFFOLK: Well hath your highness seen into this Duke,
And had I first been put to speak my mind,
I think I should have told your grace's tale.

CARDINAL: Smooth runs the water where the brook is deep,
 And in his simple show he harbours treason.

YORK: Indeed, my sovereign, Gloucester is a man
 Unsounded yet, and full of deep deceit.

KING HENRY: My lords at once: the care you have of us
 To mow down thorns that would annoy our foot
 Is worthy praise; but shall I speak my conscience,
 Our kinsman Gloucester is as innocent
 From meaning treason to our royal person
 As is the sucking lamb or harmless dove.

MARGARET: Ah, what's more dangerous than this fond
             affiance?
 Seems he a dove? His feathers are but borrowed.
 Take heed, my lord, the welfare of us all
 Hangs on the cutting short that fraudful man.

Enter DUKE HUMPHREY of Gloucester.

DUKE HUMPHREY: All happiness unto my lord the King.
 Pardon, my liege, that I have stayed so long.

SUFFOLK: Nay Gloucester, know that thou art come too soon
 Unless thou wert more loyal than thou art.
 I do arrest thee of high treason here.

DUKE HUMPHREY: Well, Suffolk's Duke, thou shalt not
             see me blush.
 Who can accuse me? Wherein am I guilty?

YORK: 'Tis thought, my lord, that you took bribes of France,
 And being Protector, stayed the soldiers' pay,
 By means whereof his highness hath lost France.

DUKE HUMPHREY: Is it but thought so? What are they
             that think it?
 I never robbed the soldiers of their pay,
 Nor ever had one penny bribe from France.

That coin that e'er I hoarded to my use
Be brought against me at the judgement day.

CARDINAL: In your Protectorship you did devise
Strange tortures for offenders, never heard of,
That England was defamed by tyranny.

DUKE HUMPHREY: Why, 'tis well known that whiles I was
Protector
Pity was all the fault that was in me.
So help me God, as I have watched the night,
Ay, night by night, in studying good for England.

SUFFOLK: My lord, these faults are easy, quickly answerèd,
But mightier crimes are laid unto your charge
Whereof you cannot easily purge yourself.
I do arrest you in his highness' name,
And here commit you to my good lord Cardinal
To keep until your further time of trial.

KING HENRY: My lord of Gloucester, 'tis my special hope
That you will clear yourself from all suspect.
My conscience tells me you are innocent.

DUKE HUMPHREY: Ah gracious lord, these days are
dangerous.
Virtue is choked with foul ambition,
And charity chased hence by rancour's hand.
Foul subornation is predominant,
And equity exiled your highness' land.
I know their complot is to have my life,
And if my death might make this island happy
And prove the period of their tyranny,
I would expend it with all willingness.
But mine is made the prologue to their play,
For thousands more that yet suspect no peril
Will not conclude their plotted tragedy.
Beaufort's red sparkling eyes blab his heart's malice,
And Suffolk's cloudy brow his stormy hate;

And doggèd York that reaches at the moon,
Whose overweening arm I have plucked back,
By false accuse doth level at my life.
And you, my sovereign lady, with the rest,
Causeless have laid disgraces on my head,
And with your best endeavour have stirred up
My liefest liege to be mine enemy.
Ay, all of you have laid your heads together –
And all to make away my guiltless life.

CARDINAL: My liege, his railing is intolerable.

SUFFOLK: Hath he not twit our sovereign lady here
    With ignominious words, though clerkly couched?

MARGARET: But I can give the loser leave to chide.

DUKE HUMPHREY: Far truer spoke than meant. I lose
                                                    indeed;
    Beshrew the winners, for they played me false.

CARDINAL: Sirs, take away the Duke and guard him sure.

DUKE HUMPHREY: Ah, thus King Henry throws away
                                            his crutch
    Before his legs be firm to bear his body.
    Thus is the shepherd beaten from thy side,
    And wolves are gnarling who shall gnaw thee first.
    Ah that my fear were false, ah that it were!
    For good King Henry, thy decay I fear.

Exit DUKE HUMPHREY, guarded by the CARDINAL's men.

KING HENRY: My lords, what to your wisdoms seemeth best
    Do or undo, as if ourself were here.

MARGARET: What, will your highness leave the Parliament?

KING HENRY: Ay Margaret, my heart is drowned with grief.
    Ah uncle Humphrey, in thy face I see
    The map of honour, truth, and loyalty;

And yet, good Humphrey, is the hour to come
That e'er I proved thee false, or feared thy faith.
What louring star now envies thy estate,
That these great lords and Margaret our Queen
Do seek subversion of thy harmless life?
Thou never didst them wrong, nor no man wrong.
And as the butcher takes away the calf,
And binds the wretch, and beats it when it strains,
Bearing it to the bloody slaughterhouse,
Even so remorseless have they borne him hence;
And as the dam runs lowing up and down,
Looking the way her harmless young one went,
And can do naught but wail her darling's loss,
Even so myself bewails good Gloucester's case
With sad unhelpful tears, and with dimmed eyes
Look after him, and cannot do him good,
So mighty are his vowèd enemies.
His fortunes I will weep, and 'twixt each groan,
Say 'Who's a traitor? Gloucester, he is none'.

Exit, attended by WARWICK.

MARGARET: Free lords, cold snow melts with the sun's hot
                                                beams.
Henry my lord is cold in great affairs,
Too full of foolish pity; believe me, lords,
This Gloucester should be quickly rid the world
To rid us from the fear we have of him.

CARDINAL: That he should die is worthy policy;
But yet we want a colour for his death.
'Tis meet he be condemned by course of law.

SUFFOLK: But in my mind that were no policy.
The King will labour still to save his life,
The commons haply rise to save his life;
So do not stand on quillets how to slay him:
Be it by gins, by snares, by subtlety,

Sleeping or waking, 'tis no matter how,
So he be dead.

MARGARET: 'Tis resolutely spoke.

SUFFOLK: Not resolute, except so much were done;
Say but the word and I will be his priest.

CARDINAL: But I would have him dead, my lord of Suffolk,
Ere you can take due orders for a priest.
Say you consent and censure well the deed,
And I'll provide his executioner;
I tender so the safety of my liege.

SUFFOLK: Here is my hand; the deed is worthy doing.

MARGARET: And so say I.

YORK: And I. And now we three have spoke it,
It skills not greatly who impugns our doom.

Enter a POST.

POST: Great lords, from Ireland am I come amain
To signify that rebels there are up
And put the Englishmen unto the sword.
Send succours, lords, and stop the rage betime.

CARDINAL: A breach that craves a quick expedient stop!
My lord of York, try what your fortune is.
To Ireland will you lead a band of men
And try your hap against the Irishmen?

YORK: I will, my lord, so please his majesty.

SUFFOLK: Why, our authority is his consent,
And what we do establish he confirms.
Then noble York, take thou this task in hand.
But now return we to the false Duke Humphrey.

CARDINAL: No more of him; for I will deal with him
That henceforth he shall trouble us no more.

YORK: My lord of Suffolk, within fourteen days
　　At Bristol I expect my soldiers;
　　From there I'll ship them all for Ireland.

SUFFOLK: I'll see it truly done, my lord of York.

Exeunt all but YORK.

YORK: Now, York, or never, be that thou hop'st to be!
　　Well, nobles, well: 'tis politicly done
　　To send me packing with an host of men.
　　'Twas men I lacked, and you will give them me.
　　I take it kindly; yet be well assured
　　You put sharp weapons in a madman's hands.
　　Whiles I in Ireland nurse a mighty band,
　　I will stir up in England some black storm
　　Shall blow ten thousand souls to heaven or hell,
　　And this fell tempest shall not cease to rage
　　Until the golden crown rests on my head.
　　And for a minister of my intent,
　　I have seduced a headstrong Kentishman,
　　John Cade of Ashford,
　　To make commotion, as full well he can,
　　Under the title of John Mortimer.
　　By this I shall perceive the commons' mind,
　　How they affect the house and claim of York.
　　Say he be taken, racked, and torturèd;
　　I know no pain they can inflict upon him
　　Will make him say I moved him to those arms.
　　Say that he thrive, as 'tis great like he will,
　　Why then from Ireland come I with my strength
　　And reap the harvest which that coistrel sowed.
　　For Humphrey being dead, as he shall be,
　　And Henry put apart, the next for me. (*Exit.*)

Interval.

Scene 8

Sound trumpets. Enter KING HENRY, MARGARET, CARDINAL, SOMERSET, and ATTENDANTS.

KING HENRY: (*To SUFFOLK.*) Go call our uncle to our
                                            presence straight.
    Say we intend to try his grace today
    If he be guilty, as 'tis publishèd.

SUFFOLK: I'll call him presently, my noble lord. (*Exit.*)

KING HENRY: Lords, take your places; and I pray you all
    Proceed no straiter 'gainst our uncle Gloucester
    Than from true evidence, of good esteem,
    He be approved in practice culpable.

MARGARET: Pray God he may acquit him of suspicion.

KING HENRY: I thank thee Meg, these words content me
                                            much.

    Enter SUFFOLK.

    How now? Why look'st thou pale? Why tremblest thou?
    Where is our uncle? What's the matter, Suffolk?

SUFFOLK: Dead in his bed, my lord: Gloucester is dead.

MARGARET: Marry, God forfend!

CARDINAL: God's secret judgement: I did dream tonight
    The Duke was dumb and could not speak a word.

    KING HENRY swoons.

MARGARET: How fares my lord? Help, lords, the King is
                                            dead.
    Run, go, help, help! O Henry, ope thine eyes.

SOMERSET: He doth revive again. Madam, be patient.

KING HENRY: O heavenly God!

MARGARET: How fares my gracious lord?

SUFFOLK: Comfort, my sovereign; gracious Henry, comfort.

KING HENRY: What, doth my lord of Suffolk comfort me?
    Came he right now to sing a raven's note
    Whose dismal tune bereft my vital powers;
    And thinks he that the chirping of a wren,
    By crying comfort from a hollow breast,
    Can chase away the first-conceivèd sound?
    Hide not thy poison with such sugared words.

He begins to rise. SUFFOLK offers to assist him.

    Lay not thy hands on me; forbear, I say.
    Their touch affrights me as a serpent's sting.
    Thou baleful messenger, out of my sight!

MARGARET: Why do you rate my lord of Suffolk thus?
    Although the Duke was enemy to him,
    Yet he most Christian-like laments his death.
    What know I how the world may deem of me,
    For it is known we were but hollow friends;
    It may be judged I made the Duke away.

KING HENRY: Ah woe is me for Gloucester, wretched man!

MARGARET: Be woe for me, more wretched than he is.
    What, dost thou turn away and hide thy face?
    I am no loathsome leper, look on me.
    Is all thy comfort shut in Gloucester's tomb?
    Why then Queen Margaret was ne'er thy joy.

Noise within. Enter WARWICK.

WARWICK: It is reported, mighty sovereign,
    That good Duke Humphrey traitorously is murdered
    By Suffolk and the Cardinal Beaufort's means.
    The commons, like an angry hive of bees
    That want their leader, scatter up and down
    And care not who they sting in his revenge.

Myself have calmed their spleenful mutiny,
Until they hear the order of his death.

KING HENRY: That he is dead, good Warwick, 'tis too true.
But how he died God knows, not Henry.
Enter his chamber, view his breathless corpse,
And comment then upon his sudden death.

WARWICK: That shall I do, my liege.

KING HENRY: O thou that judgest all things, stay my
thoughts,
My thoughts that labour to persuade my soul
Some violent hands were laid on Humphrey's life.
If my suspect be false, forgive me God,
For judgement only doth belong to thee.

Enter WARWICK.

DUKE HUMPHREY's bed is brought in.

WARWICK: Come hither, gracious sovereign, view this body.

KING HENRY: That is to see how deep my grave is made,
For with his soul fled all my worldly solace,
And seeing him I see my life in death.

WARWICK: As surely as my soul intends to live
With that dread King that took our state upon him
To free us from his father's wrathful curse,
I do believe that violent hands were laid
Upon the life of this thrice-famèd Duke.

SUFFOLK: A dreadful oath, sworn with a solemn tongue!
What instance gives Lord Warwick for his vow?

WARWICK: See how his face is black and full of blood;
His eyeballs further out than when he lived,
Staring full ghastly like a strangled man;
His hair upreared, his nostrils stretched with struggling,
His hands abroad displayed, as one that grasped

And tugged for life and was by strength subdued.
It cannot be but he was murdered here.

SUFFOLK: Why Warwick, who should do the Duke to death?
Myself and Beaufort had him in protection,
And we I hope, sir, are no murderers.

WARWICK: But both of you were vowed Duke Humphrey's
foes,
(*To CARDINAL.*) And you, forsooth, had the good Duke
to keep.
'Tis like you would not feast him like a friend;
And 'tis well seen he found an enemy.

*Exit CARDINAL, who cannot bear the sight of the body any
longer, assisted by SOMERSET.*

MARGARET: Then you belike suspect these noblemen
As guilty of Duke Humphrey's timeless death?

WARWICK: Who finds the heifer dead and bleeding fresh,
And sees fast by a butcher with an axe,
But will suspect 'twas he that made the slaughter?

MARGARET: Are you the butcher, Suffolk? Where's your
knife?

WARWICK: Madam be still, with reverence may I say,
For every word you speak in his behalf
Is slander to your royal dignity.

SUFFOLK: I wear no knife to slaughter sleeping men,
But here's a vengeful sword, rusted with ease,
That shall be scourèd in his rancorous heart
That slanders me with murder's crimson badge.
Say if thou dar'st, proud Lord of Warwickshire,
That I am faulty in Duke Humphrey's death.

WARWICK: What dares not Warwick, if false Suffolk dare him?
Pernicious blood-sucker of sleeping men!

SUFFOLK and WARWICK draw their weapons.

KING HENRY: Why how now lords, your wrathful weapons
drawn

Here in our presence? Dare you be so bold?

Enter EXETER from the commons.

EXETER: Dread lord, the commons send you word by me
Unless Lord Suffolk straight be done to death,
Or banishèd fair England's territories,
They will by violence tear him from your palace
And torture him with grievous ling'ring death.
They say, by him the good Duke Humphrey died;
They say, in him they fear your highness' death.

COMMONS: (*Within.*) An answer from the King, or we
will all break in!

KING HENRY: Go Exeter, and tell them all from me
I thank them for their tender loving care,
And had I not been 'cited so by them,
Yet did I purpose as they do entreat;
For sure my thoughts do hourly prophesy
Mischance unto my state by Suffolk's means.
And therefore by his majesty I swear,
Whose far unworthy deputy I am,
He shall not breathe infection in this air
But three days longer, on the pain of death.

Exit EXETER.

MARGARET: O Henry, let me plead for gentle Suffolk.

KING HENRY: Ungentle Queen, to call him gentle Suffolk.
No more, I say! If thou dost plead for him
Thou wilt but add increase unto my wrath.
Had I but said, I would have kept my word;
But when I swear, it is irrevocable.
(*To SUFFOLK.*) If after three days' space thou here beest
found

On any ground that I am ruler of,
The world shall not be ransom for thy life.

Enter SOMERSET.

What news, Lord Somerset?

SOMERSET: Your majesty,
    The Cardinal Beaufort is at point of death.
    For suddenly a grievous sickness took him
    That makes him gasp, and stare, and catch the air,
    Blaspheming God and cursing men on earth.
    Sometime he talks as if Duke Humphrey's ghost
    Were by his side; sometime he calls your highness,
    And whispers to his pillow, as to you,
    The secrets of his over-chargèd soul;
    And even now he cries aloud for you.

KING HENRY: Come Somerset, come Warwick, go with me.

Exeunt all but MARGARET and SUFFOLK.

MARGARET: Mischance and sorrow go along with you!
    Heart's discontent and sour affliction
    Be playfellows to keep you company!

SUFFOLK: Cease, gentle Queen, these execrations,
    And let thy Suffolk take his heavy leave.

MARGARET: Give me thy hand,
    That I may dew it with my mournful tears;
    Nor let the rain of heaven wet this place
    To wash away my woeful monuments.

She kisses his palm.

So get thee gone, that I may know my grief.
    'Tis but surmised whiles thou art standing by,
    O go not yet. Even thus two friends condemned
    Embrace, and kiss, and take ten thousand leaves,
    Loather a hundred times to part than die.
    Yet now farewell, and farewell life with thee.

SUFFOLK: Thus is poor Suffolk ten times banishèd,
    Once by the King, and three times thrice by thee.

'Tis not the land I care for, wert thou thence;
A wilderness is populous enough,
So Suffolk had thy heavenly company.
For where thou art, there is the world itself,
And where thou art not, desolation.
I can no more. Live thou to joy thy life;
Myself no joy in naught but that thou liv'st.

MARGARET: Now get thee hence. The King, thou know'st,
is coming.

If thou be found by me, thou art but dead.

SUFFOLK: If I depart from thee, I cannot live.
O let me stay, befall what may befall!

MARGARET: To France, sweet Suffolk. Let me hear from thee.
For wheresoe'er thou art in this world's globe
I'll have an Iris that shall find thee out.

SUFFOLK: I go.

MARGARET: And take my heart with thee.

She kisses him.

SUFFOLK: A jewel, locked into the woefull'st cask
That ever did contain a thing of worth.
Even as a splitted barque, so sunder we:
This way fall I to death.

MARGARET: This way for me.

As MARGARET leaves, the COMMONS pour on stage and murder SUFFOLK.

Scene 9

The CARDINAL's bedroom.

Enter the ghost of DUKE HUMPHREY to the CARDINAL in bed.

CARDINAL: If thou beest death, I'll give thee England's
treasure

Enough to purchase such another island,
So thou wilt let me live and feel no pain.

Enter KING HENRY, SOMERSET, and WARWICK.

KING HENRY: How fares my lord? Speak, Beaufort, to thy
sovereign.

The CARDINAL cries out.

Ah, what a sign it is of evil life
Where death's approach is seen so terrible.

WARWICK: Beaufort, it is thy sovereign speaks to thee.

CARDINAL: Bring me unto my trial when you will.
Died he not in his bed? Where should he die?
Can I make men live whe'er they will or no?
O torture me no more, I will confess.
Alive again?
He hath no eyes! The dust hath blinded them.
Comb down his hair – look, look, it stands upright,
Like lime twigs set to catch my wingèd soul.

KING HENRY: O thou eternal mover of the heavens,
Look with a gentle eye upon this wretch.
O beat away the busy meddling fiend
That lays strong siege unto this wretch's soul,
And from his bosom purge this black despair.

WARWICK: See how the pangs of death do make him grin.

SOMERSET: Disturb him not, let him pass peaceably.

KING HENRY: Lord Card'nal, if thou think'st on heaven's
bliss,
Hold up thy hand, make signal of thy hope.

CARDINAL dies.

He dies and makes no sign. O God forgive him.

WARWICK: So bad a death argues a monstrous life.

KING HENRY: Forbear to judge, for we are sinners all,
   And let us all to meditation.

Exeunt.

Scene 10

Blackheath, London.

Enter two REBELS with long staves.

FIRST REBEL: Come and get thee a sword, though made
   of a lath; they have been up these two days.

SECOND REBEL: They have the more need to sleep now
   then.

FIRST REBEL: I tell thee, Jack Cade the clothier means to
   dress the commonwealth, and turn it, and set a new nap
   upon it.

SECOND REBEL: So he had need, for 'tis threadbare.
   Well, I say it was never merry world in England since
   gentlemen came up.

FIRST REBEL: O miserable age! Virtue is not regarded in
   handicraftsmen.

SECOND REBEL: The nobility think scorn to go in
   leather aprons.

FIRST REBEL: Nay more, the King's Council are no good
   workmen.

SECOND REBEL: True; and yet it is said 'Labour in
   thy vocation'; which is as much to say as 'Let the
   magistrates be labouring men'; and therefore should we
   be magistrates.

FIRST REBEL: Thou hast hit it; for there's no better sign
   of a brave mind than a hard hand.

SECOND REBEL: I see them, I see them! There's Best's son, the tanner of Wingham.

FIRST REBEL: He shall have the skins of our enemies to make dog's leather of.

SECOND REBEL: And Dick the butcher.

FIRST REBEL: Then is sin struck down like an ox, and iniquity's throat cut like a calf.

SECOND REBEL: And Smith the weaver.

FIRST REBEL: Argo, their thread of life is spun.

SECOND REBEL: Come, come, let's fall in with them.

Enter Jack CADE, Dick the BUTCHER, Smith the WEAVER, with infinite numbers, all with long staves.

CADE: We, John Cade, so termed of our supposed father –

BUTCHER: (*Aside.*) Or rather of stealing a cade of herrings.

CADE: For our enemies shall fall before us, inspired with the spirit of putting down kings and princes – command silence.

BUTCHER: Silence.

CADE: My father was a Mortimer –

BUTCHER: (*Aside.*) He was an honest man and a good bricklayer.

CADE: My mother a Plantagenet –

BUTCHER: (*Aside.*) I knew her well, she was a midwife.

CADE: Therefore am I of an honourable house.

BUTCHER: (*Aside.*) Ay, by my faith, the field is honourable, and there was he born, under a hedge.

CADE: Valiant I am –

WEAVER: (*Aside.*) A must needs, for beggary is valiant.

CADE: I am able to endure much, and I fear neither sword nor fire. Be brave then, for your captain is brave and vows reformation. There shall be in England seven halfpenny loaves sold for a penny, the three-hooped pot shall have ten hoops, and I will make it felony to drink small beer. All the realm shall be in common, and in Cheapside shall my palfrey go to grass; and when I am king, as king I will be –

ALL FOLLOWERS: God save your majesty!

CADE: I thank you good people – there shall be no money, all shall eat and drink on my score, and I will apparel them all in one livery that they may agree like brothers, and worship me their lord.

BUTCHER: The first thing we do, let's kill all the lawyers.

CADE: Nay, that I mean to do. How now? Who's there?

Enter some with the CLERK of Chatham.

WEAVER: The Clerk of Chatham: he can write and read and cast account.

CADE: I am sorry for't. The man is a proper man, of mine honour. Unless I find him guilty, he shall not die. Come hither, sirrah, I must examine thee. What is thy name?

CLERK: Emmanuel.

CADE: Dost thou use to write thy name? Or hast thou a mark to thyself like an honest plain-dealing man?

CLERK: Sir, I thank God I have been so well brought up that I can write my name.

ALL FOLLOWERS: He hath confessed – away with him! He's a villain and a traitor.

CADE: Away with him, I say, hang him with his pen and inkhorn about his neck.

Exit one with the CLERK.

Enter a REBEL.

REBEL: Where's our general?

CADE: Here I am, thou particular fellow.

REBEL: Fly, fly, fly! Sir Humphrey Stafford is hard by with the King's forces.

CADE: Stand, villain, stand, or I'll fell thee down. He shall be encountered with a man as good as himself. He is but a knight, is a?

REBEL: No.

CADE: To equal him I will make myself a knight presently.

He kneels and knights himself.

Rise up, Sir John Mortimer.

He rises.

Now have at him!

Enter Sir Humphrey STAFFORD, attended.

STAFFORD: Rebellious hinds, the filth and scum of Kent,
Marked for the gallows, lay your weapons down;
Home to your cottages, forsake this groom.
The King is merciful, if you revolt,
But angry, wrathful, and inclined to blood,
If you go forward, therefore yield or die.

CADE: As for these silken-coated slaves, I pass not.
It is to you, good people, that I speak,
Over whom, in time to come, I hope to reign,
For I am rightful heir unto the crown.

STAFFORD: Villain, thy father was a plasterer,
    And thou thyself a shearman, art thou not?

CADE: And Adam was a gardener.

STAFFORD: And what of that?

CADE: Marry, this: Edmund Mortimer, Earl of March,
    Married the Duke of Clarence' daughter, did he not?

STAFFORD: Ay, sir.

CADE: By her he had two children at one birth.

STAFFORD: That's false.

CADE: Ay, there's the question; but I say 'tis true.
    The elder of them, being put to nurse,
    Was by a beggar-woman stol'n away,
    And ignorant of his birth and parentage,
    Became a bricklayer when he came to age.
    His son am I, deny it if you can.

BUTCHER: Nay, 'tis too true, therefore he shall be king.

WEAVER: Sir, he made a chimney in my father's house,
    and the bricks are alive at this day to testify it. Therefore
    deny it not.

STAFFORD: And will you credit this base drudge's words
    That speaks he knows not what?

ALL FOLLOWERS: Ay, marry will we, therefore get ye gone.

STAFFORD: Jack Cade, the Duke of York hath taught you
    this.

CADE: Go to, sirrah, tell the King from me that for his
    father's sake, Henry the Fifth, I am content he shall
    reign, but I'll be Protector over him.

BUTCHER: And furthermore, we'll have the Lord Saye's
    head for selling the dukedom of Maine.

CADE: And good reason, for thereby is England maimed,
and fain to go with a staff, but that my puissance holds it
up. Fellow-kings, I tell you that that Lord Saye hath
gelded the commonwealth, and made it an eunuch, and
more than that, he can speak French, and therefore he is
a traitor.

STAFFORD: O gross and miserable ignorance!

CADE: Nay, answer if you can. The Frenchmen are our
enemies; go to, then, I ask but this: can he that speaks
with the tongue of an enemy be a good counsellor or no?

ALL FOLLOWERS No, no, and therefore we'll have his
head!

STAFFORD: Herald away, and throughout every town
Proclaim them traitors that are up with Cade,
That those which fly before the battle ends
May even in their wives' and children's sight,
Be hanged up for example at their doors;
And you that be the King's friends, follow me!

Exeunt STAFFORD and his SOLDIERS.

CADE: And you that love the commons, follow me!
Now show yourselves men, 'tis for liberty.
We will not leave one lord, one gentleman:
Spare none but such as go in clouted shoon.

BUTCHER: They are all in order, and march toward us.

CADE: But then are we in order when we are most out of
order. Come, march forward!

*Alarums to the fight, wherein STAFFORD is slain. CADE
puts on STAFFORD's uniform and loots the body.*

This monument of the victory will I bear, and the body
shall be dragged at my horse heels till I do come to
London, where we will have the Mayor's sword borne
before us.

BUTCHER: If we mean to thrive and do good, break open
the jails and let out the prisoners.

CADE: Fear not that, I warrant thee. Come, let's march
towards London.

Exeunt, dragging STAFFORD's body.

Scene 11

The Royal Palace.

*Enter KING HENRY with a supplication, and MARGARET with
SUFFOLK's head.*

MARGARET: Oft have I heard that grief softens the mind,
And makes it fearful and degenerate;
Think therefore on revenge, and cease to weep.
But who can cease to weep and look on this?
Here may his head lie on my throbbing breast,
But where's the body that I should embrace?

Enter SOMERSET and Lord SAYE.

SOMERSET: What answer makes your grace to the rebels'
supplication?

KING HENRY: I'll send some holy bishop to entreat,
For God forbid so many simple souls
Should perish by the sword. And I myself,
Rather than bloody war shall cut them short,
Will parley with Jack Cade their general.
Lord Saye, Jack Cade hath sworn to have thy head.

SAYE: Ay, but I hope your highness shall have his.

KING HENRY: How now, madam?
Still lamenting and mourning Suffolk's death?
I fear me, love, if that I had been dead,
Thou wouldest not have mourned so much for me.

MARGARET: No my love, I should not mourn, but die for thee.

Enter a REBEL.

REBEL: The rebels are in Southwark. Fly, my lords!
    Jack Cade proclaims himself Lord Mortimer,
    And vows to crown himself in Westminster.
    All scholars, lawyers, courtiers, gentlemen,
    We call false caterpillars and intend their death. (*Exit.*)

KING HENRY: O graceless men, they know not what they do.

SOMERSET: My gracious lord, retire to Kenilworth
    Until a power be raised to put them down.

MARGARET: Ah, were the Duke of Suffolk now alive
    These Kentish rebels would be soon appeased!

KING HENRY: Lord Saye, the traitors hateth thee,
    Therefore away with us to Kenilworth.

SAYE: So might your grace's person be in danger.
    And therefore in this city will I stay
    And live alone as secret as I may.

KING HENRY: Come Margaret, God our hope will
                       succour us.

MARGARET: (*Aside.*) My hope is gone, now Suffolk is deceased.

KING HENRY: (*To SAYE.*) Farewell, my lord, trust not the
                       Kentish rebels.

SOMERSET: (*To SAYE.*) Trust nobody, for fear you be
                       betrayed.

SAYE: The trust I have is in mine innocence,
    And therefore am I bold and resolute.

Exeunt.

Scene 12

Enter CADE and the rest. CADE strikes his staff on London Stone.

CADE: Now is Mortimer lord of this city. And here sitting upon London Stone, I charge and command, that of the city's cost the Pissing Conduit run nothing but claret wine this first year of our reign. And now henceforward it shall be treason for any that calls me other than Lord Mortimer.

Enter a SOLDIER, searching for CADE.

SOLDIER: Jack Cade, Jack Cade!

CADE: Knock him down there.

They kill him.

WEAVER: If this fellow be wise, he'll never call ye Jack Cade more; I think he hath a very fair warning.

REBEL: My lord, a prize, a prize! Here's the Lord Saye which sold the towns in France.

Enter a REBEL with SAYE.

CADE: Well, he shall be beheaded for it ten times. (*To SAYE.*) Ah thou say, thou serge, nay, thou buckram lord! What canst thou answer to my majesty for giving up of Normandy unto Mounsieur Buss-my-cue, the Dolphin of France? Be it known unto thee by these presence, even the presence of Lord Mortimer, that I am the besom that must sweep the court clean of such filth as thou art. Thou hast most traitorously corrupted the youth of the realm in erecting a grammar school; and whereas before, our forefathers had no other books but the score and the tally, thou hast caused printing to be used, and contrary to the King his crown and dignity, thou hast built a paper-mill. It will be proved to thy face that thou hast men about thee that usually talk of a noun and a verb and such abominable words as no Christian ear can endure to hear. Thou hast appointed justices of peace to call poor men before them about matters they were not able to answer. Moreover, thou hast put them in prison, and because they could not read, thou hast hanged them, when indeed only for that cause they have been most worthy to live.

SAYE: You men of Kent.

BUTCHER: What say you of Kent?

SAYE: Nothing but this: 'tis *bona terra, mala gens.*

CADE: Away with him, away with him, he speaks Latin.

SAYE: Hear me but speak, and bear me where you will.
  I sold not Maine, I lost not Normandy;
  Yet to recover them would lose my life.
  Justice with favour have I always done,
  Prayers and tears have moved me, gifts could never.
  When have I aught exacted at your hands,
  But to maintain the King, the realm, and you?
  These cheeks are pale with watching for your good –

CADE: Give him a box o'th' ear, and that will make 'em red
                                                     again.

SAYE: Long sitting to determine poor men's causes
  Hath made me full of sickness and diseases.

CADE: Let's see if his head will stand steadier on a pole or no. Go, take him away, and strike off his head presently; and then break into his son-in-law's house, Sir James Cromer, and strike off his head, and bring them both upon two poles hither.

ALL FOLLOWERS It shall be done.

  Exeunt one or two with SAYE.

CADE: The proudest peer in the realm shall not wear a head on his shoulders unless he pay me tribute. There shall not a maid be married but she shall pay to me her maidenhead, ere they have it. Married men shall hold of me *in capite*. And we charge and command that their wives be as free as heart can wish or tongue can tell.

Enter two with SAYE's head and Sir James CROMER's upon two poles.

Is not this brave? Let them kiss one another, for they loved well when they were alive.

The two heads are made to kiss.

Now part them again, lest they consult about the giving up of some more towns in France. Now go some and pull down th'Inns of Court, down with them all. Away, burn all the records of the realm. My mouth shall be the Parliament of England. Go and set London bridge on fire, and if you can, burn down the tower too. Up Fish Street! Down Saint Magnus' Corner! Kill and knock down!

Sound a parley.

What noise is this I hear? Dare any be so bold to sound retreat or parley when I command them kill?

Enter Old Lord CLIFFORD and YOUNG CLIFFORD.

CLIFFORD: Ay, here they be that dare and will disturb thee!
  Know, Cade, we come ambassadors from the King
  Unto the commons, whom thou hast misled,
  And here pronounce free pardon to them all
  That will forsake thee and go home in peace.

YOUNG CLIFFORD What say ye, countrymen, will ye relent
  And yield to mercy whilst 'tis offered you,
  Or let a rebel lead you to your deaths?
  Who loves the King and will embrace his pardon,
  Fling up his cap and say 'God save his majesty'.
  Who hateth him and honours not his father,

Henry the Fifth, that made all France to quake,
Shake he his weapon at us, and pass by.

They forsake CADE.

ALL FOLLOWERS: God save the King! God save the King!

CADE: What, my lords Clifford, are ye so brave? And you,
base peasants, do ye believe him? Will you needs be
hanged with your pardons about your necks? You are all
recreants and dastards, and delight to live in slavery to
the nobility. Let them break your backs with burdens,
take your houses over your heads, ravish your wives and
daughters before your faces.

ALL FOLLOWERS: We'll follow Cade! We'll follow Cade!

They run to CADE again.

CLIFFORD: Is Cade the son of Henry the Fifth
That thus you do exclaim you'll go with him?
Will he conduct you through the heart of France
And make the meanest of you earls and dukes?
Alas, he hath no home, no place to fly to,
Nor knows he how to live but by the spoil,
Unless by robbing of your friends and us.

ALL FOLLOWERS: A Clifford! A Clifford! We'll follow
the King and Clifford!

They forsake CADE.

CADE: (*Aside.*) Was ever feather so lightly blown to and fro
as this multitude? The name of Henry the Fifth hales
them to an hundred mischiefs, and makes them leave me
desolate. My sword make way for me, for here is no
staying. And heavens and honour be witness that no want
of resolution in me, but only my followers' base and
ignominious treasons, makes me betake me to my heels.
(*Aloud.*) In despite of the devils and hell, have through
the very middest of you.

He fights his way out.

CLIFFORD: What, is he fled? Go some, and follow him,
    And he that brings his head unto the King
    Shall have a thousand crowns for his reward.

Exeunt some of them after CADE.

(*To the remaining REBELS.*) Follow me, soldiers, we'll
                            devise a mean

To reconcile you all unto the King.

Exeunt.

Scene 13

St Albans.

Enter YORK and his army of Irish.

YORK: From Ireland thus comes York to claim his right,
    And pluck the crown from feeble Henry's head.
    Ring bells aloud, burn bonfires clear and bright,
    To entertain great England's lawful king.

*Enter KING HENRY, MARGARET, SOMERSET, and
ATTENDANTS.*

KING HENRY: Now York, what means these forces thou
                                 dost bring?

YORK: To heave the traitor Somerset from hence.

KING HENRY: That is too much presumption on thy part.

YORK: Shall I endure the sight of Somerset?
    Now York, unloose thy long imprisoned thoughts:
    Henry of Lancaster, thou art not king;
    Not fit to govern and rule multitudes,
    Which dar'st not – no, nor canst not – rule a traitor.
    That head of thine doth not become a crown;
    Thy hand is made to grasp a palmer's staff,

And not to grace an aweful princely sceptre.
That gold must round engird these brows of mine.
Here is a hand to hold a sceptre up,
And with the same to act controlling laws.
Give place! By heaven, thou shalt rule no more
O'er him whom heaven created for thy ruler.

SOMERSET: O monstrous traitor! I arrest thee, York,
Of capital treason 'gainst the King and crown.

YORK: (*To an ATTENDANT.*) Sirrah, call in my sons to be
my bail.

Exit ATTENDANT.

MARGARET: (*To an attendant.*) Call hither Clifford, bid
him come amain,
To say if that the bastard boys of York
Shall be the surety for their traitor father.

Exit ATTENDANT.

*Enter YORK's sons EDWARD, GEORGE, and crookback
RICHARD with SOLDIERS.*

YORK: See where they come, I'll warrant they'll make it good.

Enter CLIFFORD and his son, with SOLDIERS.

MARGARET: And here comes Clifford to deny their bail.

CLIFFORD: (*Kneeling before KING HENRY.*) Health and all
happiness to my lord the King.

He rises.

YORK: We are thy sovereign, Clifford, kneel again.
For thy mistaking so, we pardon thee.

CLIFFORD: This is my king, York; I do not mistake.
(*To KING HENRY.*) To Bedlam with him! Is the man
grown mad?

KING HENRY: Ay Clifford, a bedlam and ambitious humour
    Makes him oppose himself against his king.

CLIFFORD: He is a traitor; let him to the Tower,
    And chop away that factious pate of his.

MARGARET: He is arrested, but will not obey.
    His sons, he says, shall give their words for him.

YORK: Will you not, sons?

EDWARD: Ay noble father,

GEORGE: If our words will serve.

RICHARD: And if words will not, then our weapons shall.

CLIFFORD: Why, what a brood of traitors have we here!

YORK: Look in a glass, and call thy image so.
    I am thy king, and thou a false-heart traitor.
    Call hither to the stake my true brave bear,
    That with the very shaking of his chains,
    He may astonish these fell-lurking curs.

Enter WARWICK with SOLDIERS.

KING HENRY: Why Warwick, hath thy knee forgot to bow?

WARWICK: My lord, I have considered with myself
    The title of this most renownèd Duke,
    And in my conscience do repute his grace
    The rightful heir to England's royal seat.

KING HENRY: Hast thou not sworn allegiance unto me?

WARWICK: I have.

KING HENRY: Canst thou dispense with heaven for such
                              an oath?

WARWICK: It is great sin to swear unto a sin,
    But greater sin to keep a sinful oath.

MARGARET: A subtle traitor needs no sophister.

YOUNG CLIFFORD: And so to arms, victorious father,
    To quell the rebels and their complices.

RICHARD: Fie, charity, for shame! Speak not in spite,
    For you shall sup with Jesu Christ tonight.

SOMERSET: Foul stigmatic, that's more than thou canst tell.

RICHARD: If not in heaven, you'll surely sup in hell.

YORK: Now Lancaster, sit sure; thy sinews shrink.
    Yield up thy crown unto the house of York!

Exeunt all but YORK and CLIFFORD.

Alarums to the battle.

CLIFFORD: What seest thou in me, York? Why dost thou
                                                    pause?

YORK: With thy brave bearing should I be in love,
    But that thou art so fast mine enemy.

CLIFFORD: Nor should thy prowess want praise and esteem,
    But that 'tis shown ignobly and in treason.

YORK: So let it help me now against thy sword,
    As I in justice and true right express it.

CLIFFORD: My soul and body on the action both.

Alarms. They fight, and YORK kills CLIFFORD.

YORK: Thus war hath given thee peace, for thou art still.
    Peace with his soul, heaven, if it be thy will. (*Exit.*)

Alarums, then enter YOUNG CLIFFORD.

YOUNG CLIFFORD: Shame and confusion, all is on the rout!
    Fear frames disorder, and disorder wounds
    Where it should guard.

He sees his father's body.

O let the vile world end,
And the premisèd flames of the last day
Knit earth and heaven together. Even at this sight
My heart is turned to stone, and while 'tis mine
It shall be stony. York not our old men spares;
No more will I their babes.
Henceforth I will not have to do with pity.
In cruelty will I seek out my fame.

Exit with the body.

Alarums.

Enter RICHARD and SOMERSET. They fight. SOMERSET is slain.

RICHARD: So lie thou there, my lord of Somerset.
Sword, hold thy temper; heart, be wrathful still;
Priests pray for enemies, but princes kill.

Exit with the body.

Alarums still. Enter KING HENRY, MARGARET, and others.

MARGARET: Away my lord, you are slow, for shame away!

KING HENRY: Can we outrun the heavens? Good
Margaret, stay.

MARGARET: What are you made of? You'll nor fight nor fly.
Now is it manhood, wisdom, and defence,
To give the enemy way, and to secure us
By what we can, which can no more but fly.

Alarum afar off.

If you be ta'en, we then should see the bottom
Of all our fortunes; but if we haply scape –
As well we may if not through your neglect –
We shall to London get where you are loved,
And where this breach now in our fortunes made
May readily be stopped.

Enter YOUNG CLIFFORD.

YOUNG CLIFFORD: (*To KING HENRY.*) But that my
heart's on future mischief set,
I would speak blasphemy ere bid you fly;
But fly you must, away my lord, away!

Exeunt.

Enter the Yorkists.

WARWICK: Now by my sword, well hast thou fought today.

YORK: By th' mass, so did we all.

RICHARD: (*Throwing down SOMERSET's head.*) Speak thou
for me, and tell them what I did.

YORK: Richard hath best deserved of all my sons.
What, is your grace dead, my lord of Somerset?

WARWICK: But we have not yet got what we would have.
'Tis not enough our foes are this time fled,
Being opposites of such repairing nature.

YORK: I know our safety is to follow them,
For as I hear, the King is fled to London.
To call a present court of Parliament.
What says Lord Warwick, shall we after them?

WARWICK: After them? Nay, before them if we can.
Now by my hand, lords, 'twas a glorious day.
Saint Albans battle won by famous York
Shall be eternized in all age to come.
Sound drums and trumpets, and to London all,
And more such days as these to us befall!

Flourish. Exeunt.

End of Part One.

PART TWO

Scene 14

Alarum. Enter YORK, his three sons EDWARD, GEORGE, and RICHARD, and WARWICK, with soldiers. They all wear white roses in their hats.

WARWICK: This is the palace of the fearful King,
　　　And this the regal seat: possess it, York,
　　　For this is thine, and not King Henry's heirs'.

YORK: Assist me then, sweet Warwick, and I will.
　　　Soldiers, conceal yourselves.

　　　The SOLDIERS withdraw, ready for an ambush.

　　　Today Queen Margaret holds her Parliament,
　　　But little thinks we shall be of her council.

WARWICK: 'The Bloody Parliament' shall this be called,
　　　Unless Plantagenet, Duke of York, be king.
　　　I'll plant Plantagenet, root him up who dares.
　　　Resolve thee, Richard – claim the English crown.

　　　YORK sits on the throne.

　　　Flourish. Enter KING HENRY, YOUNG CLIFFORD, EXETER, and the rest. They all wear red roses in their hats.

KING HENRY: My lords, look where the sturdy rebel sits
　　　Even in the chair of state! Belike he means,
　　　Backed by the power of Warwick, that false peer,
　　　To aspire unto the crown and reign as king.

CLIFFORD: He durst not sit there had your father lived.
　　　My gracious lord, here in the Parliament
　　　Let us assail the family of York.

KING HENRY: Far be the thought of this from Henry's heart,
　　　To make a shambles of the Parliament House.

Cousin of Exeter, frowns, words, and threats
Shall be the war that Henry means to use.
Thou factious Duke of York, descend my throne
And kneel for grace and mercy at my feet.
I am thy sovereign.

YORK: I am thine.

EXETER: Thy father was a traitor to the crown.

WARWICK: Exeter, thou art a traitor to the crown
    In following this usurping Henry.

CLIFFORD: Whom should he follow but his natural king?

WARWICK: True, Clifford, and that's Richard Duke of York.

YORK: (*To KING HENRY.*) Will you we show our title to
                                    the crown?

KING HENRY: What title hast thou, traitor, to the crown?
    Thy father was as thou art Duke of York;
    I am the son of Henry the Fifth,
    Who made the Dauphin and the French to stoop
    And seized upon their towns and provinces.

WARWICK: Talk not of France, sith thou hast lost it all.

KING HENRY: My title's good, and better far than his.

WARWICK: Prove it, Henry, and thou shalt be king.

KING HENRY: Henry the Fourth by conquest got the crown.

YORK: 'Twas by rebellion against his king.

KING HENRY: Tell me, may not a king adopt an heir?

YORK: What then?

KING HENRY: An if he may, then am I lawful king,
    For Richard, in the view of many lords,
    Resigned the crown to Henry the Fourth,
    Whose heir my father was, and I am his.

YORK: He rose against him, being his sovereign,
    And made him to resign his crown perforce.

CLIFFORD: King Henry, be thy title right or wrong,
    Lord Clifford vows to fight in thy defence.
    May that ground gape and swallow me alive
    Where I shall kneel to him that slew my father.

WARWICK: Do right unto this princely Duke of York,
    Or I will fill the house with armèd men
    And over the chair of state, where now he sits,
    Write up his title with usurping blood.

He stamps with his foot and the SOLDIERS show themselves.

KING HENRY: My lord of Warwick, hear me but one word:
    Let me for this my lifetime reign as king.

YORK: Confirm the crown to me and to mine heirs,
    And thou shalt reign in quiet while thou liv'st.

KING HENRY: I am content. Richard Plantagenet,
    Enjoy the kingdom after my decease.

CLIFFORD: What wrong is this unto the prince your son?
    I go, to tell the Queen these news.
    Farewell, faint-hearted and degenerate king,
    In whose cold blood no spark of honour bides.

Exit with his SOLDIERS.

KING HENRY: Ah, Exeter.

WARWICK: Why should you sigh, my lord?

KING HENRY: Not for myself, Lord Warwick, but my son,
    Whom I unnaturally shall disinherit.
    But be it as it may. (*To YORK.*) I here entail
    The crown to thee and to thine heirs for ever,
    Conditionally, that here thou take thine oath
    To cease this civil war, and whilst I live
    To honour me as thy king and sovereign.

YORK: This oath I willingly take and will perform.

WARWICK: Long live King Henry. (*To YORK.*) Plantagenet,
embrace him.

YORK descends. KING HENRY and YORK embrace.

KING HENRY: (*To YORK.*) And long live thou, and these
thy forward sons.

YORK: Now York and Lancaster are reconciled.

EXETER: Accursed be he that seeks to make them foes.

YORK: Farewell, my gracious lord, I'll to my castle.

*Exeunt YORK, EDWARD, GEORGE, and RICHARD, with
SOLDIERS.*

WARWICK: And I'll keep London with my soldiers.

Exit with SOLDIERS.

KING HENRY and EXETER turn to leave.

Enter MARGARET and PRINCE EDWARD.

EXETER: Here comes the Queen, whose looks bewray her
anger.

I'll steal away.

KING HENRY: Exeter, so will I.

MARGARET: Nay, go not from me, I will follow thee.

KING HENRY: Be patient, gentle Queen, and I will stay.

MARGARET: Who can be patient in such extremes?
Ah wretched man, would I had died a maid
And never seen thee, never borne thee son,
Seeing thou hast proved so unnatural a father.
Hath he deserved to lose his birthright thus?
Hadst thou but loved him half so well as I,
Or felt that pain which I did for him once,

Or nourished him as I did with my blood,
Thou wouldst have left thy dearest heart-blood there
Rather than have made that savage Duke thine heir
And disinherited thine only son.

PRINCE EDWARD: Father, you cannot disinherit me.
If you be king, why should not I succeed?

KING HENRY: Pardon me, Margaret; pardon me, sweet son,
The Earl of Warwick and the Duke enforced me.

MARGARET: Enforced thee? Art thou king, and wilt be forced?
I shame to hear thee speak! Ah timorous wretch,
Thou hast undone thyself, thy son, and me,
And giv'n unto the house of York such head
As thou shalt reign but by their sufferance.
Had I been there, which am a silly woman,
The soldiers should have tossed me on their pikes
Before I would have granted to that act.
But thou preferr'st thy life before thine honour.
And seeing thou dost, I here divorce myself
Both from thy table, Henry, and thy bed,
Until that act of Parliament be repealed
Whereby my son is disinherited.
The northern lords that have forsworn thy colours
Will follow mine, if once they see them spread,
And spread they shall be, to thy foul disgrace
And utter ruin of the house of York.
Thus do I leave thee.
(*To PRINCE EDWARD.*) Come, son, let's away.
Our army is ready; come, we'll after them.

KING HENRY: Stay, gentle Margaret, and hear me speak.

MARGARET: Thou hast spoke too much already, get thee
gone.

KING HENRY: Gentle son Edward, thou wilt stay with me?

MARGARET: Ay, to be murdered by his enemies.

PRINCE EDWARD: When I return with victory from the
field,
    I'll see your grace. Till then, I'll follow her.

MARGARET: Come son, away, we may not linger thus.

    Exit with PRINCE EDWARD.

KING HENRY: Poor Queen, how love to me and to her son
    Hath made her break out into terms of rage.
    Go cousin, and entreat them to a peace.

EXETER: And I, I hope, shall reconcile you all.

    Exeunt severally.

Scene 15

YORK's castle near Wakefield.

Enter RICHARD, EDWARD, GEORGE, and RUTLAND.

RICHARD: Brother, though I be youngest, give me leave.

EDWARD: No, I can better play the orator.

GEORGE: But I have reasons strong and forcible.

    Enter YORK.

YORK: What is your quarrel, who began it first?

EDWARD: No quarrel, but a slight contention.

YORK: About what?

RUTLAND: About the crown of England, which is yours.

YORK: Mine, boy? Not till King Henry be dead.

RICHARD: Your right depends not on his life or death.

YORK: I took an oath that he should quietly reign.

GEORGE: But for a kingdom any oath may be broken.

EDWARD: I would break a thousand oaths to reign one year.

RICHARD: No, God forbid your grace should be forsworn.

YORK: I shall be if I claim by open war.

RICHARD: I'll prove the contrary, if you'll hear me speak.

YORK: Thou canst not, son; it is impossible.

RICHARD: An oath is of no moment being not took
    Before a true and lawful magistrate
    That hath authority over him that swears.
    Henry had none, but did usurp the place.
    Then seeing 'twas he that made you to depose,
    Your oath, my lord, is vain and frivolous.
    Therefore to arms; and father, do but think
    How sweet a thing it is to wear a crown,
    Within whose circuit is Elysium
    And all that poets feign of bliss and joy.
    Why do we linger thus? I cannot rest
    Until the white rose that I wear be dyed
    Even in the luke-warm blood of Henry's heart.

YORK: Richard, enough. I will be king or die.

Enter a MESSENGER.

    But stay, what news?

MESSENGER: The Queen, with all the northern earls and
                                                    lords,
    Intend here to besiege you in your castle.
    She is hard by with twenty thousand men.

YORK: So much for simple Henry and his oaths.

A march sounds afar off.

EDWARD: I hear their drums. Let's set our men in order,
    And issue forth and bid them battle straight.

YORK: Five men to twenty: though the odds be great,
    I doubt not of a noble victory.
    Many a battle have I won in France
    Whenas the enemy hath been ten to one.
    Why should I not now have the like success?

RICHARD: A woman's general – what should we fear?

Exeunt all but RUTLAND.

Enter CLIFFORD with SOLDIERS.

RUTLAND: Ah see where bloody Clifford comes,
    And whither shall I fly to scape his hand?

CLIFFORD: Here is the brat of this accursèd Duke
    Whose father slew my father; he shall die.

RUTLAND: Ah Clifford, murder not this innocent child
    Lest thou be hated both of God and man.

RUTLAND closes his eyes.

CLIFFORD: How now, is he dead already? Or is it fear
    That makes him close his eyes? I'll open them.

RUTLAND: O gentle Clifford, kill me with thy sword
    And not with such a cruel threat'ning look.
    Sweet Clifford, hear me speak before I die.
    I am too mean a subject for thy wrath.
    Be thou revenged on men, and let me live.

CLIFFORD: In vain thou speak'st, poor boy. My father's
                                                    blood
    Hath stopped the passage where thy words should enter.

RUTLAND: Then let my father's blood open it again.
    He is a man, and Clifford, cope with him.

CLIFFORD: Had I thy brethren here, their lives and thine
    Were not revenge sufficient for me.

RUTLAND: O let me pray before I take my death.
　　To thee I pray: sweet Clifford, pity me.

CLIFFORD: Such pity as my rapier's point affords.

RUTLAND: I never did thee harm; why wilt thou slay me?

CLIFFORD: Thy father slew my father, therefore die.

He stabs him, and he dies.

Plantagenet, I come, Plantagenet!
And this thy son's blood cleaving to my blade
Shall rust upon my weapon till thy blood,
Congealed with this, do make me wipe off both.

Exit with RUTLAND's body and SOLDIERS.

Scene 16

Alarum. Enter YORK.

YORK: The army of the Queen hath got the field;
　　And all my followers to the eager foe
　　Turn back and fly like ships before the wind,
　　Or lambs pursued by hunger-starvèd wolves.
　　My sons – God knows what hath bechancèd them.

A short alarum within.

Ah hark, the fatal followers do pursue,
And I am faint and cannot fly their fury;
The sands are numbered that makes up my life.
Here must I stay, and here my life must end.

Enter MARGARET, CLIFFORD, EXETER, and PRINCE EDWARD, with SOLDIERS.

MARGARET: Yield to our mercy, proud Plantagenet.

CLIFFORD: Ay, to such mercy as he showed my father.

They take YORK prisoner.

EXETER: What would your grace have done unto him now?

MARGARET: Come make him stand upon this molehill here,
    That wrought at mountains with outstretchèd arms
    Yet parted but the shadow with his hand.
    What, was it you that would be England's king?
    Was't you that revelled in our Parliament,
    And made a preachment of your high descent?
    Where are your mess of sons to back you now,
    The wanton Edward and the lusty George?
    And where's that valiant crookback prodigy,
    Dickie your boy, that with his grumbling voice
    Was wont to cheer his dad in mutinies?
    Or with the rest where is your darling Rutland?
    Look, York, I stained this napkin with the blood
    That valiant Clifford with his rapier's point
    Made issue from the bosom of the boy.
    And if thine eyes can water for his death,
    I give thee this to dry thy cheeks withal.
    Alas poor York, but that I hate thee deadly
    I should lament thy miserable state.
    I prithee grieve, to make me merry, York.
    What, hath thy fiery heart so parched thine entrails
    That not a tear can fall for Rutland's death?
    Why art thou patient, man? Thou shouldst be mad,
    And I, to make thee mad, do mock thee thus.
    Stamp, rave, and fret, that I may sing and dance.
    Thou wouldst be fee'd, I see, to make me sport.
    York cannot speak unless he wear a crown.
    A crown for York, and lords, bow low to him.
    Hold you his hands whilst I do set it on.
    Ay marry, sirs, now looks he like a king.
    Ay, this is he that took King Henry's chair,
    And this is he was his adopted heir.
    But how is it that great Plantagenet
    Is crowned so soon and broke his solemn oath?
    As I bethink me, you should not be king

Till our King Henry had shook hands with death.
O 'tis a fault too too unpardonable.
Off with the crown, and with the crown his head,
And whilst we breathe, take time to do him dead.

CLIFFORD: That is my office for my father's sake.

MARGARET: Nay, stay – let's hear the orisons he makes.

YORK: She-wolf of France, but worse than wolves of France,
How ill-beseeming is it in thy sex
To triumph like an Amazonian trull
Upon their woes whom fortune captivates!
But that thy face is visor-like, unchanging,
Made impudent with use of evil deeds,
I would essay, proud Queen, to make thee blush.
O tiger's heart wrapped in a woman's hide!
How couldst thou drain the life-blood of the child
To bid the father wipe his eyes withal,
And yet be seen to bear a woman's face?
Women are soft, mild, pitiful, and flexible;
Thou stern, obdurate, flinty, rough, remorseless.
Bidd'st thou me rage? Why now thou hast thy wish.
Wouldst have me weep? Why now thou hast thy will.
These tears are my sweet Rutland's obsequies,
And every drop cries vengeance for his death
'Gainst thee, fell Clifford, and thee, false Frenchwoman.
That face of his the hungry cannibals
Would not have touched, would not have stained with blood.
See, ruthless Queen, a hapless father's tears.
This cloth thou dipped'st in blood of my sweet boy,
And I with tears do wash the blood away.
Keep thou the napkin and go boast of this.
There, take the crown, and with the crown, my curse:
And in thy need such comfort come to thee
As now I reap at thy too cruel hand.

EXETER: Had he been slaughter-man to all my kin,
I should not, for my life, but weep with him.

MARGARET: What, weeping-ripe, my lord of Exeter?
    Think but upon the wrong he did us all,
    And that will quickly dry thy melting tears.

CLIFFORD: Here's for my oath, here's for my father's death.

He stabs YORK.

MARGARET: And here's to right our gentle-hearted King.

She stabs YORK.

YORK: Open thy gate of mercy, gracious God:
    My soul flies through these wounds to seek out thee. (*He dies.*)

MARGARET: Off with his head and set it on York gates,
    So York may overlook the town of York.

Flourish. Exeunt with YORK's body.

Scene 17

A march. Enter EDWARD, GEORGE and RICHARD, and their power.

EDWARD: I wonder how our princely father scaped,
    Or whether he be scaped away or no.
    Had he been ta'en we should have heard the news;
    Had he been slain we should have heard the news.
    How fares my brother? Why is he so sad?

RICHARD: I cannot joy until I be resolved
    Where our right valiant father is become.
    I saw him in the battle ringed about,
    As is a bear encompassed round with dogs,
    Who having pinched a few and made them cry,
    The rest stand all aloof and bark at him:
    So fared our father with his enemies.
    Methinks 'tis prize enough to be his son.

Enter one blowing.

But what art thou whose heavy looks foretell
Some dreadful story hanging on thy tongue?

MESSENGER: Ah, one that was a woeful looker-on
Whenas the noble Duke of York was slain.

EDWARD: O speak no more, for I have heard too much.

RICHARD: Say how he died, for I will hear it all.

MESSENGER: Environèd he was with many foes,
But only slaughtered by the ireful arm
Of unrelenting Clifford and the Queen,
Who crowned the gracious Duke in high despite,
Laughed in his face, and when with grief he wept,
The ruthless Queen gave him to dry his cheeks
A napkin steepèd in the harmless blood
Of sweet young Rutland, by rough Clifford slain;
And after many scorns, many foul taunts,
They took his head, and on the gates of York
They set the same; and there it doth remain.

EDWARD: O Clifford, boist'rous Clifford, thou hast slain
The flower of Europe for his chivalry.

GEORGE: Never, O never shall I see more joy.

RICHARD: I cannot weep, for all my body's moisture
Scarce serves to quench my furnace-burning heart.
To weep is to make less the depth of grief:
Tears then for babes, blows and revenge for me.
Richard, I bear thy name; I'll venge thy death.

March. Enter WARWICK and his army.

WARWICK: How now, fair lords? What fare? What news
abroad?

RICHARD: O valiant lord, the Duke of York is slain.

WARWICK: Ten days ago I drowned these news in tears.
And now post-haste am come to join with you,

Making another head to fight again.
Attend me, lords. The proud insulting Queen
Has wrought the easy-melting King like wax.
He swore consent to your succession,
His oath enrollèd in the Parliament.
But now to London Margaret is gone,
To frustrate both his oath and what beside
May make against the house of Lancaster.
So *via*, to London will we march,
And once again cry 'Charge!' upon our foes.

EDWARD: Lord Warwick, on thy shoulder will I lean.

WARWICK: Then King of England shalt thou be proclaimed
In every borough as we pass along.
Stay we no longer dreaming of renown,
But sound the trumpets and about our task.

A distant alarm.

How now? What new alarum is this same?

RICHARD: The Queen is coming with a puissant host.

WARWICK: Why then it sorts. Brave warriors, let's away.

EDWARD: Then strike up drums – God and Saint George
for us!

March. Exeunt.

Scene 18

*Flourish. Enter KING HENRY, MARGARET, CLIFFORD,
EXETER, and young PRINCE EDWARD, with SOLDIERS.*

MARGARET: Welcome, my lord, to this brave town of York.
Yonder's the head of that arch-enemy
That sought to be encompassed with your crown.
Doth not the object cheer your heart, my lord?

KING HENRY: To see this sight, it irks my very soul.
    Withhold revenge, dear God, 'tis not my fault,
    Nor wittingly have I infringed my vow.

CLIFFORD: My gracious liege, this too much lenity
    And harmful pity must be laid aside.
    Ambitious York did level at thy crown;
    He but a duke, would have his son a king,
    Thou being a king, blest with a goodly son,
    Didst yield consent to disinherit him,
    Which argued thee a most unloving father.
    Were it not pity that this goodly boy
    Should lose his birthright by his father's fault,
    And long hereafter say unto his child
    'What my great-grandfather and grandsire got
    My careless father fondly gave away'?

KING HENRY: But Clifford, tell me, didst thou never hear
    That things ill got had ever bad success?
    I'll leave my son my virtuous deeds behind,
    And would my father had left me no more.
    Ah cousin York, would thy best friends did know
    How it doth grieve me that thy head is here.

MARGARET: My lord, cheer up your spirits, our foes are nigh,
    And this soft courage makes your followers faint.
    You promised knighthood to our forward son.
    Unsheathe your sword and dub him presently.
    Edward, kneel down.

KING HENRY: Edward Plantagenet, arise a knight,
    And learn this lesson: draw thy sword in right.

PRINCE EDWARD: My gracious father, by your kingly leave,
    I'll draw it as apparent to the crown,
    And in that quarrel use it to the death.

CLIFFORD: Why, that is spoken like a toward prince.

Enter a MESSENGER.

MESSENGER: Royal commanders, be in readiness,
  For with a band of thirty thousand men
  Comes Warwick backing Edward, Duke of York;
  And in the towns as they do march along,
  Proclaims him king, and many fly to him.
  Array your battle, for they are at hand.

CLIFFORD: I would your highness would depart the field;
  The Queen hath best success when you are absent.

MARGARET: Ay good my lord, and leave us to our fortune.

KING HENRY: Why that's my fortune too, therefore I'll stay.

MARGARET: Be it with resolution then to fight.

March. Enter EDWARD, WARWICK, RICHARD,
GEORGE, and SOLDIERS.

EDWARD: Now, perjured Henry, wilt thou kneel for grace,
  And set thy diadem upon my head,
  Or bide the mortal fortune of the field?

MARGARET: Go rate thy minions, proud insulting boy!
  Becomes it thee to be thus bold in terms
  Before thy sovereign and thy lawful king?

EDWARD: I am his king, and he should bow his knee.
  I was adopted heir by his consent.

GEORGE: Since when his oath is broke; for as I hear,
  You that are king, though he do wear the crown,
  Have caused him by new act of Parliament
  To blot our brother out, and put his own son in.

CLIFFORD: And reason too –
  Who should succeed the father but the son?

RICHARD: Are you there, butcher? O, I cannot speak!

CLIFFORD: Ay crookback, here I stand to answer thee,
  Or any he the proudest of thy sort.

RICHARD: 'Twas you that killed young Rutland, was it not?

CLIFFORD: Ay, and old York, and yet not satisfied.

RICHARD: For God's sake, lords, give signal to the fight.

KING HENRY: Have done, my lords, and hear me speak.

MARGARET: Defy them then, or else hold close thy lips.

KING HENRY: I prithee give no limits to my tongue;
I am a king, and privileged to speak.

CLIFFORD: My liege, the wound that bred this meeting here
Cannot be cured by words, therefore be still.

EDWARD: Since thou deniest the gentle King to speak,
Sound trumpets, let our bloody colours wave!
And either victory, or else a grave!

MARGARET: Stay, Edward.

EDWARD: No wrangling woman, we'll no longer stay,
These words will cost ten thousand lives this day.

Flourish. Exeunt all but RICHARD and CLIFFORD.

The Battle of Towton begins.

Alarums. Excursions.

RICHARD: Now Clifford, I have singled thee alone.
Suppose this arm is for the Duke of York,
And this for Rutland, both bound to revenge.

CLIFFORD: Now Richard, I am with thee here alone.
This is the hand that stabbed thy father York,
And this the hand that slew thy brother Rutland,
And here's the heart that triumphs in their death
And cheers these hands that slew thy sire and brother
To execute the like upon thyself –
And so, have at thee!

They fight. Enter WARWICK. CLIFFORD flies.

RICHARD: Nay, Warwick, single out some other chase,
    For I myself will hunt this wolf to death.

Exeunt.

Alarum. Enter KING HENRY alone.

KING HENRY: This battle fares like to the morning's war,
    When dying clouds contend with growing light,
    What time the shepherd, blowing of his nails,
    Can neither call it perfect day nor night.
    Now sways it this way like a mighty sea
    Forced by the tide to combat with the wind,
    Now sways it that way like the selfsame sea
    Forced to retire by fury of the wind.
    Sometime the flood prevails, and then the wind;
    Now one the better, then another best –
    Both tugging to be victors, breast to breast,
    Yet neither conqueror nor conquerèd.
    So is the equal poise of this fell war.
    Here on this molehill will I sit me down.
    To whom God will, there be the victory.
    For Margaret my queen, and Clifford too,
    Have chid me from the battle, swearing both
    They prosper best of all when I am thence.
    O God! Methinks it were a happy life
    To be no better than a homely swain.
    To sit upon a hill, as I do now,
    To carve out dials quaintly, point by point,
    Thereby to see the minutes how they run:
    So many hours must I tend my flock,
    So many hours must I take my rest,
    So many hours must I contemplate,
    So many hours must I sport myself,
    So many days my ewes have been with young,
    So many weeks ere the poor fools will ean,
    So many years ere I shall shear the fleece.
    So minutes, hours, days, weeks, months, and years,

Passed over to the end they were created,
Would bring white hairs unto a quiet grave.
Ah, what a life were this! How sweet! How lovely!
Gives not the hawthorn bush a sweeter shade
To shepherds looking on their silly sheep
Than doth a rich embroidered canopy
To kings that fear their subjects' treachery?
O yes it doth, a thousandfold it doth.
And to conclude, the shepherd's homely curds,
His cold thin drink out of his leather bottle,
His wonted sleep under a fresh tree's shade,
All which secure and sweetly he enjoys,
Is far beyond a prince's delicates,
His viands sparkling in a golden cup,
His body couchèd in a curious bed,
When care, mistrust, and treason waits on him.

*Alarum. Enter at one side a SON that has killed his father,
and at another a FATHER that has killed his son. They carry
bodies in their arms.*

SON: This man, whom hand to hand I slew in fight,
    May be possessèd with some store of crowns.

FATHER: Thou that so stoutly hath resisted me,
    Give me thy gold, if thou hast any gold,
    For I have bought it with an hundred blows.
    But let me see: is this our foeman's face?

SON: Who's this? O God! It is my father's face.

FATHER: Ah no, no, no, it is mine only son!
    Ah boy, if any life be left in thee,
    Throw up thine eye!

SON: O heavy times, begetting such events!

FATHER: O pity, God, this miserable age!

SON: From London by the King was I pressed forth;
    My father being the Earl of Warwick's man,

Came on the part of York, pressed by his master;
And I, who at his hands received my life,
Have by my hands of life bereavèd him.

FATHER: What stratagems, how fell, how butcherly,
Erroneous, mutinous, and unnatural,
This deadly quarrel daily doth beget!
O boy, thy father gave thee life too soon,
And hath bereft thee of thy life too late!

SON: Pardon me, God, I knew not what I did;
And pardon father, for I knew not thee.
My tears shall wipe away these bloody marks,
And no more words till they have flowed their fill.

KING HENRY: O piteous spectacle! O bloody times!
Whiles lions war and battle for their dens,
Poor harmless lambs abide their enmity.
Weep, wretched man, I'll aid thee tear for tear;
And let our hearts and eyes, like civil war,
Be blind with tears, and break, o'ercharged with grief.
O pity, pity, gentle heaven, pity!
The red rose and the white are on his face,
The fatal colours of our striving houses;
Wither one rose, and let the other flourish;
If you contend, a thousand lives must wither.

SON: How will my mother for a father's death
Take on with me, and ne'er be satisfied!

FATHER: How will my wife for slaughter of my son
Shed seas of tears, and ne'er be satisfied!

KING HENRY: How will the country for these woeful chances
Misthink the King, and not be satisfied!

SON: Was ever son so rued a father's death?

FATHER: Was ever father so bemoaned his son?

KING HENRY: Was ever king so grieved for subjects' woe?

SON: I'll bear thee hence where I may weep my fill.
　　For I have murdered where I should not kill.

SON exits with the body of his father.

FATHER: I'll bear thee hence, and let them fight that will,
　　For I have murdered where I should not kill.

FATHER exits with the body of his son.

KING HENRY: Sad-hearted men, much overgone with care,
　　Here sits a king more woeful than you are.

Alarums. Excursions. Enter MARGARET, PRINCE EDWARD, and EXETER.

PRINCE EDWARD: Fly father, fly, for all your friends are fled.

EXETER: Now Warwick rages like a chafèd bull!

MARGARET: Away, for death doth hold us in pursuit!

Exeunt.

A loud alarum. Enter CLIFFORD, wounded.

CLIFFORD: Here burns my candle out, ay here it dies,
　　Which whiles it lasted, gave King Henry light.
　　O Lancaster, I fear thy overthrow
　　More than my body's parting with my soul!
　　The foe is merciless and will not pity,
　　For at their hands I have deserved no pity.
　　Come York and Richard, Warwick and the rest –
　　I stabbed your father's bosom, split my breast.

He faints.

Alarum and retreat. Enter EDWARD, his brothers GEORGE and RICHARD, WARWICK, and SOLDIERS.

EDWARD: Now breathe we, lords, good fortune bids us pause,
　　And smoothe the frowns of war with peaceful looks.
　　Some troops pursue the bloody-minded Queen;
　　But think you, lords, that Clifford fled with them?

WARWICK: No, 'tis impossible he should escape;
    Your brother Richard marked him for the grave.
    And whereso'er he is, he's surely dead.

CLIFFORD groans and then faints again.

RICHARD: Whose soul is that which takes her heavy leave?

EDWARD: See who it is, and now the battle's ended,
    If friend or foe, let him be gently used.

*RICHARD revives and then strangles CLIFFORD during
this next speech.*

RICHARD: Revoke that doom of mercy, for 'tis Clifford,
    Who not contented that he lopped the branch
    In hewing Rutland when his leaves put forth,
    But set his murd'ring knife unto the root
    From whence that tender spray did sweetly spring,
    I mean our princely father, Duke of York.

CLIFFORD dies.

Thou didst love York, and I am son to York.

EDWARD: Thou pitied'st Rutland, I will pity thee.

GEORGE: Where's Captain Margaret to fence you now?

WARWICK: From off the gates of York fetch down the head,
    Your father's head, which Clifford placèd there.
    Instead whereof let this supply the room:
    Measure for measure must be answerèd.
    And now to London with triumphant march,
    There to be crownèd England's royal king;
    From whence shall Warwick cut the sea to France,
    And ask the Lady Bona for thy queen:
    So shalt thou sinew both these lands together.

EDWARD: Even as thou wilt, sweet Warwick, let it be.
    For never will I undertake the thing
    Wherein thy counsel and consent is wanting.

Richard, I will create thee Duke of Gloucester,
And George of Clarence; Warwick, as ourself,
Shall do and undo as him pleaseth best.

RICHARD: Let me be Duke of Clarence, George of
Gloucester,

For Gloucester's dukedom is too ominous.

WARWICK: Tut, that's a foolish observation:
Richard, be Duke of Gloucester. Now to London
To see these honours in possession.

*Exeunt all but KING HENRY, watched by two Yorkist
SOLDIERS.*

KING HENRY: Now Harry, England is no land of thine.
Thy place is filled, thy sceptre wrung from thee,
Thy balm washed off wherewith thou wast anointed.
No bending knee will call thee Caesar now,
No humble suitors press to speak for right,
No, not a man comes for redress of thee –
For how can I help them and not myself?
My queen and son are gone to France for aid,
And as I hear, the great commanding Warwick
Is thither gone to crave the French King's sister
To wife for Edward. If this news be true,
Poor Queen and son, your labour is but lost;
For Warwick is a subtle orator,
And Louis a prince soon won with moving words.
By this account, then, Margaret may win him,
For she's a woman to be pitied much.
Ay, but she's come to beg, Warwick to give.

FIRST SOLDIER: Say, what art thou that talk'st of kings
and queens?

KING HENRY: More than I seem, and less than I was born to:
A man at least, for less I should not be;
And men may talk of kings, and why not I?

SECOND SOLDIER: Ay, but thou talk'st as if thou wert a
king.

KING HENRY: Why, so I am in mind, and that's enough.

FIRST SOLDIER: But if thou be a king, where is thy crown?

KING HENRY: My crown is in my heart, not on my head,
Not decked with diamonds and Indian stones,
Nor to be seen. My crown is called content:
A crown it is that seldom kings enjoy.

SECOND SOLDIER: Well, if you be a king crowned with
content,
Your crown content and you must be contented
To go along with us, for as we think,
You are the king King Edward hath deposed.

FIRST SOLDIER: And we his subjects sworn in all allegiance
Will apprehend you as his enemy.

KING HENRY: But did you never swear and break an oath?

SECOND SOLDIER: No, never such an oath, nor will not now.

KING HENRY: Where did you dwell when I was King of
England?

FIRST SOLDIER: Here in this country, where we now
remain.

KING HENRY: I was anointed king at nine months old,
And you were sworn true subjects unto me:
And tell me then, have you not broke your oaths?

SECOND SOLDIER: No, for we were subjects but while
you were king.

KING HENRY: Why, am I dead? Do I not breathe a man?
Ah simple men, you know not what you swear.
Look as I blow this feather from my face,
And as the air blows it to me again,

Obeying with my wind when I do blow,
And yielding to another when it blows,
Commanded always by the greater gust:
Such is the lightness of you common men.
But do not break your oaths, for of that sin
My mild entreaty shall not make you guilty.

FIRST SOLDIER: We charge you in God's name and in the
King's,

To go with us unto the officers.

KING HENRY: In God's name, lead; your king's name be
obeyed;

And what God will, that let your king perform;
And what he will I humbly yield unto.

Exeunt.

Scene 19

The Royal Palace at Westminster.

Enter King EDWARD, RICHARD, now Duke of Gloucester, George, now Duke of CLARENCE, and the LADY GREY.

EDWARD: Brother of Gloucester, at Saint Albans field
This lady's husband, Sir Richard Grey, was slain,
His lands then seized on by the conqueror.
Her suit is now to repossess those lands,
Which we in justice cannot well deny,
Because in quarrel of the house of York
The worthy gentleman did lose his life.

RICHARD: Your highness shall do well to grant her suit;
It were dishonour to deny it her.

EDWARD: It were no less, but yet I'll make a pause.

RICHARD: (*Aside to CLARENCE.*) Yea, is it so?
I see the lady hath a thing to grant
Before the King will grant her humble suit.

CLARENCE: (*Aside to RICHARD.*) Silence.

EDWARD: Widow, we will consider of your suit;
　　And come some other time to know our mind.

LADY GREY: Right gracious lord, I cannot brook delay.
　　May it please your highness to resolve me now,
　　And what your pleasure is shall satisfy me.

EDWARD: How many children hast thou, widow? Tell me.

LADY GREY: Three, my most gracious lord.

RICHARD: (*Aside.*) You shall have four, an you'll be ruled
　　　　　　　　　　　　　　　　　　　　by him.

EDWARD: 'Twere pity they should lose their father's lands.

LADY GREY: Be pitiful, dread lord, and grant it them.

EDWARD: Lords, give us leave; I'll try this widow's wit.

　　RICHARD and CLARENCE stand apart.

　　Now tell me, madam, do you love your children?

LADY GREY: Ay, full as dearly as I love myself.

EDWARD: And would you not do much to do them good?

LADY GREY: To do them good I would sustain some harm.

EDWARD: Then get your husband's lands, to do them good.

LADY GREY: Therefore I came unto your majesty.

EDWARD: I'll tell you how these lands are to be got.

LADY GREY: So shall you bind me to your highness' service.

EDWARD: What service wilt thou do me, if I give them?

LADY GREY: What you command, that rests in me to do.

EDWARD: But you will take exceptions to my boon.

LADY GREY: No, gracious lord, except I cannot do it.

EDWARD: Ay, but thou canst do what I mean to ask.

LADY GREY: Why then, I will do what your grace commands.
  Why stops my lord? Shall I not hear my task?

EDWARD: An easy task, 'tis but to love a king.

LADY GREY: That's soon performed, because I am a subject.

EDWARD: Why then, thy husband's lands I freely give thee.

LADY GREY: I take my leave, with many thousand thanks.

EDWARD: But stay thee, 'tis the fruits of love I mean.

LADY GREY: The fruits of love *I* mean, my loving liege.

EDWARD: Ay, but I fear me in another sense.
  What love think'st thou I sue so much to get?

LADY GREY: My love till death, my humble thanks, my
                                                    prayers:
  That love which virtue begs and virtue grants.

EDWARD: No, by my troth, I did not mean such love.

LADY GREY: Why then, you mean not as I thought you did.

EDWARD: But now you partly may perceive my mind.

LADY GREY: My mind will never grant what I perceive
  Your highness aims at, if I aim aright.

EDWARD: To tell thee plain, I aim to lie with thee.

LADY GREY: To tell *you* plain, I had rather lie in prison.

EDWARD: Why then thou shalt not have thy husband's lands.

LADY GREY: Why then mine honesty shall be my dower;
  For by that loss I will not purchase them.

EDWARD: Therein thou wrong'st thy children mightily.

LADY GREY: Herein your highness wrongs both them and me.
  But mighty lord, this merry inclination

Accords not with the sadness of my suit.
Please you dismiss me either with ay or no.

EDWARD: Ay, if thou wilt say 'ay' to my request;
No, if thou dost say 'no' to my demand.

LADY GREY: Then no, my lord; my suit is at an end.

RICHARD: The widow likes him not, she knits her brows.

CLARENCE: He is the bluntest wooer in Christendom.

EDWARD: One way or other, she shall be my love.
(*To LADY GREY.*) Say that King Edward take thee for his
queen?

LADY GREY: 'Tis better said than done, my gracious lord.
I am a subject fit to jest withal,
But far unfit to be a sovereign.

EDWARD: Sweet widow, by my state I swear to thee
I speak no more than what my soul intends,
And that is to enjoy thee for my love.

LADY GREY: And that is more than I will yield unto.
I know I am too mean to be your queen,
And yet too good to be your concubine.

EDWARD: You cavil, widow, I did mean my queen.

LADY GREY: 'Twill grieve your grace my sons should call
you father.

EDWARD: No more than when my daughters call thee mother.
Thou art a widow and thou hast some children;
And by God's mother, I being but a bachelor,
Have other some. Why, 'tis a happy thing
To be the father unto many sons.
Answer no more, for thou shalt be my queen.
Brothers, you muse what chat we two have had.

RICHARD: The widow likes it not, for she looks very sad.

EDWARD: You'd think it strange if I should marry her.

CLARENCE: To who, my lord?

EDWARD: Why, Clarence, to myself.

RICHARD: That would be ten days' wonder at the least.

CLARENCE: That's a day longer than a wonder lasts.

RICHARD: By so much is the wonder in extremes.

EDWARD: Well jest on, brothers, I can tell you both
     Her suit is granted for her husband's lands.

Enter a MESSENGER.

MESSENGER: My gracious lord, Henry your foe is taken
     And brought as prisoner to your palace gate.

EDWARD: See that he be conveyed unto the Tower;
     And go we, brothers, to the man that took him,
     To question of his apprehension.
     Widow, go you along. Lords, use her honourably.

Exeunt all but RICHARD.

RICHARD: Ay, Edward will use women honourably.
     Would he were wasted, marrow, bones, and all,
     That from his loins no hopeful branch may spring
     To cross me from the golden time I look for.
     And yet between my soul's desire and me –
     The lustful Edward's title burièd –
     Is Clarence, Henry, and his son young Edward,
     And all the unlooked-for issue of their bodies:
     A cold premeditation for my purpose.
     Well, say there is no kingdom then for Richard;
     What other pleasure can the world afford?
     I'll make my heaven in a lady's lap,
     And deck my body in gay ornaments,
     And 'witch sweet ladies with my words and looks.
     O miserable thought! And more unlikely
     Than to accomplish twenty golden crowns.
     Why, love forswore me in my mother's womb,

And for I should not deal in her soft laws,
She did corrupt frail nature with some bribe
To shrink mine arm up like a withered shrub,
To make an envious mountain on my back,
To shape my legs of an unequal size,
To disproportion me in every part,
Like to a chaos or an unlicked bear whelp
That carries no impression like the dam.
And am I then a man to be beloved?
O monstrous fault, to harbour such a thought!
Then since this earth affords no joy to me
But to command, to check, to o'erbear such
As are of better person than myself,
I'll make my heaven to dream upon the crown,
And whiles I live, t'account this world but hell,
Until my misshaped trunk that bears this head
Be round impalèd with a glorious crown.
And yet I know not how to get the crown,
For many lives stand between me and home.
And I, like one lost in a thorny wood,
That rends the thorns and is rent with the thorns,
Seeking a way and straying from the way,
Not knowing how to find the open air,
But toiling desperately to find it out,
Torment myself to catch the English crown.
And from that torment I will free myself,
Or hew my way out with a bloody axe.
Why, I can smile, and murder whiles I smile,
And cry 'Content!' to that which grieves my heart,
And wet my cheeks with artificial tears,
And frame my face to all occasions.
I can add colours to the chameleon,
Change shapes with Proteus for advantages,
And set the murderous Machiavel to school.
Can I do this, and cannot get a crown?
Tut, were it farther off, I'll pluck it down. (*Exit.*)

Interval.

Scene 20

France. The court of KING LOUIS.

Flourish. Enter KING LOUIS of France, his sister the LADY BONA, PRINCE EDWARD, MARGARET, and EXETER. KING LOUIS takes his place on the throne.

KING LOUIS: Fair Queen of England, worthy Margaret,
    Sit down with us. It ill befits thy state
    And birth that thou shouldst stand while Louis doth sit.

MARGARET: No, mighty King of France, now Margaret
    Must strike her sail and learn a while to serve
    Where kings command. I was, I must confess,
    Great Albion's queen in former golden days,
    But now mischance hath trod my title down.

KING LOUIS: Be plain, Queen Margaret, and tell thy grief.
    It shall be eased if France can yield relief.

MARGARET: Those gracious words revive my drooping
                          thoughts,
    And give my tongue-tied sorrows leave to speak.
    Now therefore be it known to noble Louis
    That Henry is become a banished man,
    While proud ambitious Edward, Duke of York,
    Usurps the regal title and the seat
    Of England's true-anointed lawful King.
    This is the cause that I, poor Margaret,
    With this my son, Prince Edward, Henry's heir,
    Am come to crave thy just and lawful aid,
    And if thou fail us all our hope is done.

Enter WARWICK.

    But see where comes the breeder of my sorrow,
    For this is he that moves both wind and tide.

KING LOUIS: What's he approacheth boldly to our presence?

MARGARET: Our Earl of Warwick, Edward's greatest friend.

KING LOUIS: Welcome brave Warwick, what brings thee
to France?

WARWICK: From worthy Edward, King of Albion,
My lord and sovereign, and thy vowèd friend,
I come in kindness and unfeignèd love,
First to do greetings to thy royal person,
And then to crave a league of amity,
And lastly to confirm that amity
With nuptial knot, if thou vouchsafe to grant
The virtuous Lady Bona, thy fair sister,
To England's King in lawful marriage.

MARGARET: (*Aside.*) If that go forward, Henry's hope is done.

WARWICK: (*To LADY BONA.*) And gracious madam, in our
King's behalf
I am commanded, with your leave and favour,
Humbly to kiss your hand, and with my tongue
To tell the passion of my sovereign's heart,
Where fame, late ent'ring at his heedful ears,
Hath placed thy beauty's image and thy virtue.

MARGARET: King Louis and Lady Bona, hear me speak
Before you answer Warwick. His demand
Springs not from Edward's well-meant honest love,
But from deceit, bred by necessity.
For how can tyrants safely govern home
Unless abroad they purchase great alliance?

WARWICK: Injurious Margaret.

PRINCE EDWARD: And why not 'Queen'?

WARWICK: Because thy father Henry did usurp,
And thou no more art prince than she is queen.

KING LOUIS: Queen Margaret, Prince Edward, and Exeter,
Vouchsafe at our request to stand aside
While I use further conference with Warwick.

MARGARET: Heavens grant that Warwick's words bewitch
him not.

KING LOUIS: Now, Warwick, tell me even upon thy
conscience,
Is Edward your true king? For I were loath
To link with him that were not lawful chosen.

WARWICK: Thereon I pawn my credit and mine honour.

KING LOUIS: But is he gracious in the people's eye?

WARWICK: The more that Henry was unfortunate.

KING LOUIS: Then further, all dissembling set aside,
Tell me for truth the measure of his love
Unto our sister Bona.

WARWICK: Such it seems
As may beseem a monarch like himself.

KING LOUIS: (*To LADY BONA.*) Now sister, let us hear
your firm resolve.

LADY BONA: Your grant, or your denial, shall be mine.
(*To WARWICK.*) Yet I confess that often ere this day,
When I have heard your king's desert recounted,
Mine ear hath tempted judgement to desire.

KING LOUIS: (*To WARWICK.*) Then Warwick, thus: our
sister shall be Edward's.
Draw near, Queen Margaret, and be a witness
That Bona shall be wife to the English king.

PRINCE EDWARD: To Edward, but not to the English king.

MARGARET: Deceitful Warwick, it was thy device
By this alliance to make void my suit!
Before thy coming Louis was Henry's friend.

KING LOUIS: And still is friend to him and Margaret.
But if your title to the crown be weak,

As may appear by Edward's good success,
Then 'tis but reason that I be released
From giving aid which late I promisèd.
Yet shall you have all kindness at my hand
That your estate requires and mine can yield.

WARWICK: Henry having nothing, nothing can he lose.
And as for you yourself, our quondam queen,
You have a father able to maintain you,
And better 'twere you troubled him than France.

MARGARET: Peace, impudent and shameless Warwick, peace!
Proud setter-up and puller-down of kings!
I will not hence till with my talk and tears,
Both full of truth, I make King Louis behold
Thy sly conveyance and thy lord's false love,
For both of you are birds of selfsame feather.

Enter a POST.

POST: My lord ambassador, these letters are for you,
These from our King unto your majesty;
And madam, these for you, from whom I know not.

They all read their letters.

EXETER: I like it well that our fair Queen and mistress
Smiles at her news, while Warwick frowns at his.

PRINCE EDWARD: Nay, mark how Louis stamps as he
were nettled.
I hope all's for the best.

KING LOUIS: Warwick, what are thy news? And yours,
fair Queen?

MARGARET: Mine, such as fill my heart with unhoped joys.

WARWICK: Mine, full of sorrow and heart's discontent.

KING LOUIS: What, has your king married the Lady Grey?
And now to soothe your forgery and his,

Sends me a paper to persuade me patience?
Is this th'alliance that he seeks with France?
Dare he presume to scorn us in this manner?

MARGARET: I told your majesty as much before:
This proveth Edward's love and Warwick's honesty.

WARWICK: King Louis, I here protest in sight of heaven
That I am clear from this misdeed of Edward's,
No more my king, for he dishonours me,
And to repair my honour, lost for him,
I here renounce him and return to Henry.
My noble Queen, let former grudges pass,
And henceforth I am thy true servitor.
I will revenge his wrong to Lady Bona
And replant Henry in his former state.

MARGARET: Warwick, these words have turned my hate to
love,
And I forgive and quite forget old faults,
And joy that thou becom'st King Henry's friend.

WARWICK: So much his friend, ay, his unfeignèd friend,
That if King Louis vouchsafe to furnish us
With some few bands of chosen soldiers,
I'll undertake to land them on our coast
And force the tyrant from his seat by war.
'Tis not his new-made bride shall succour him.

KING LOUIS: Then England's messenger, return in post
And tell false Edward, thy supposèd king,
That Louis of France is sending over masquers
To revel it with him and his new bride.
Thou seest what's passed, go fear thy king withal.

LADY BONA: Tell him, in hope he'll prove a widower shortly,
I'll wear the willow garland for his sake.

MARGARET: Tell him my mourning weeds are laid aside,
And I am ready to put armour on.

WARWICK: Tell him from me that he hath done me wrong,
    And therefore I'll uncrown him ere't be long.

Exit POST.

KING LOUIS: Now, Warwick, thou and Exeter, with five
                                thousand men,
    Shall cross the seas and bid false Edward battle;
    And as occasion serves, this noble Queen
    And Prince shall follow with a fresh supply.
    Yet ere thou go, but answer me one doubt:
    What pledge have we of thy firm loyalty?

WARWICK: This shall assure my constant loyalty:
    That if our Queen and this young Prince agree,
    I'll join mine eldest daughter and my joy
    To him forthwith in holy wedlock bands.

MARGARET: With all my heart, and thank you for your
                                  motion.
    Son Edward, she is fair and virtuous.

PRINCE EDWARD: And here to pledge my vow I give my
                                  hand.

He and WARWICK clasp hands.

KING LOUIS: Why stay we now? These soldiers shall be
                                  levied.
    I long till Edward fall by war's mischance
    For mocking marriage with a dame of France.

Exeunt all but WARWICK.

WARWICK: I came from Edward as ambassador,
    But I return his sworn and mortal foe.
    Had he none else to make a stale but me?
    Then none but I shall turn his jest to sorrow.
    I was the chief that raised him to the crown,
    And I'll be chief to bring him down again.

Not that I pity Henry's misery,
But seek revenge on Edward's mockery. (*Exit.*)

Scene 21

London. The Royal Palace.

Enter RICHARD and CLARENCE.

RICHARD: Now tell me, brother Clarence, what think you
    Of this new marriage with the Lady Grey?
    Hath not our brother made a worthy choice?

CLARENCE: Alas, you know 'tis far from hence to France;
    How could he stay till Warwick made return?

RICHARD: Here comes the King and his well-chosen bride.

    *Flourish. Enter KING EDWARD, the LADY GREY his
    Queen, and the Lord RIVERS.*

CLARENCE: I mind to tell him plainly what I think.

EDWARD: Now, brother of Clarence, how like you our choice,
    That you stand pensive, as half-malcontent?

CLARENCE: As well as Louis of France, or the Earl of Warwick,
    Which are so weak of courage and in judgement
    That they'll take no offence at our abuse.

EDWARD: Suppose they take offence without a cause,
    They are but Louis and Warwick; I am Edward,
    Your king and Warwick's, and must have my will.

RICHARD: And you shall have your will, because our king.
    Yet hasty marriage seldom proveth well.

EDWARD: Yea, brother Richard, are you offended too?

RICHARD: Not I, no – God forbid that I should wish them
                                                severed
    Whom God hath joined together. Ay, and 'twere pity
    To sunder them that yoke so well together.

EDWARD: Setting your scorns and your mislike aside,
    Tell me some reason why the Lady Grey
    Should not become my wife and England's queen.

CLARENCE: Then this is my opinion: that King Louis
    Becomes your enemy for mocking him
    About the marriage of the Lady Bona.

RICHARD: And Warwick, doing what you gave in charge,
    Is now dishonourèd by this new marriage.

EDWARD: What if both Louis and Warwick be appeased
    By such invention as I can devise?

CLARENCE: Yet to have joined with France in such alliance
    Would more have strengthened this our commonwealth
    'Gainst foreign storms than any home-bred marriage.

RIVERS: Why, knows not Clarence that of itself
    England is safe, if true within itself?

CLARENCE: But the safer when 'tis backed with France.

RIVERS: 'Tis better using France than trusting France.
    Let us be backed with God and with the seas
    Which he hath giv'n for fence impregnable.
    In them and in ourselves our safety lies.

CLARENCE: For this one speech Lord Rivers well deserves
    To have the heir and daughter of Lord Scales.

EDWARD: Ay, what of that? It was my will and grant,
    And for this once my will shall stand for law.

RICHARD: And yet methinks your grace hath not done well
    To give her to the brother of your bride.
    She better would have fitted me or Clarence.

CLARENCE: But in your bride you bury brotherhood.

EDWARD: Alas, poor Clarence, is it for a wife
    That thou art malcontent? I will provide thee.

CLARENCE: In choosing for yourself you showed your
judgement,
Which being shallow, you shall give me leave
To play the broker in mine own behalf,
And to that end I shortly mind to leave you.

EDWARD: Leave me or tarry, Edward will be king,
And not be tied unto his brother's will.

LADY GREY: My lords, before it pleased his majesty
To raise my state to title of a queen,
Do me but right, and you must all confess
That I was not ignoble of descent,
And meaner than myself have had like fortune.
But as this title honours me and mine,
So your dislikes, to whom I would be pleasing,
Doth cloud my joys with danger and with sorrow.

EDWARD: My love, forbear to fawn upon their frowns.
What danger or what sorrow can befall thee
So long as Edward is thy constant friend,
And their true sovereign, whom they must obey?
Nay, whom they shall obey, and love thee too,
Unless they seek for hatred at my hands.

RICHARD: (*Aside.*) I hear, yet say not much, but think the
more.

Enter the POST from France.

EDWARD: Now messenger, what news from France?
What answer makes King Louis unto our letters?

POST: At my depart these were his very words:
'Go tell false Edward, thy supposèd king,
That Louis of France is sending over masquers
To revel it with him and his new bride.'

EDWARD: Is Louis so brave? Belike he thinks me Henry.
But what said Warwick to my marriage?

POST: He, more incensed against your majesty
  Than all the rest, discharged me with these words:
  'Tell him from me that he hath done me wrong,
  And therefore I'll uncrown him ere't be long.'

EDWARD: Ha! Durst the traitor breathe out so proud words?
  Well, I will arm me, being thus forewarned.
  They shall have wars and pay for their presumption.
  But say, is Warwick friends with Margaret?

POST: Ay, gracious sovereign, they are so linked in friendship
  That young Prince Edward marries Warwick's daughter.

CLARENCE: Belike the elder; Clarence will have the
               younger.
  Now brother King, farewell, and sit you fast,
  For I will hence to Warwick's other daughter,
  That though I want a kingdom, yet in marriage
  I may not prove inferior to yourself.
  You that love me and Warwick, follow me. (*Exit.*)

EDWARD: Yet am I armed against the worst can happen,
  Now, brother Richard, will you stand by us?

RICHARD: Ay, in despite of all that shall withstand you.

EDWARD: Why so, then am I sure of victory.
  We'll forward towards Warwick and his mates.
  For well I wot that Henry is no soldier.
  Ah treach'rous Clarence, how evil it beseems thee
  To flatter Henry and forsake thy brother!
  Now therefore let us hence and lose no hour
  Till we meet Warwick with his foreign power.

 Exeunt EDWARD and RICHARD.

RIVERS: These news, I must confess, are full of grief.
  Yet gracious sister, bear it as you may.
  Warwick may lose as well as win the day.

LADY GREY: Till then fair hope must hinder life's decay,
  And I the rather wean me from despair

For love of Edward's offspring in my womb.
I'll hence forthwith unto the sanctuary,
To save at least the heir of Edward's right.
There shall I rest secure from force and fraud.
Come therefore, brother Rivers, let us fly,
If Warwick take us, we are sure to die.

Exeunt.

Scene 22

Enter WARWICK and EXETER in England with French SOLDIERS.

WARWICK: Trust me my lord, all hitherto goes well.

Enter CLARENCE with SOLDIERS.

And see where George of Clarence sweeps along.
Speak suddenly my lord, are we all friends?

CLARENCE: Fear not that, my lord.

WARWICK: Then welcome Clarence; I hold it cowardice
To rest mistrustful where a noble heart
Hath pawned an open hand in sign of love,
Else might I think that Clarence, Edward's brother,
Were but a feignèd friend to our proceedings.
But welcome sweet Clarence, my daughter shall be thine.

Enter EDWARD, RICHARD, and SOLDIERS.

O unbid spite, is sportful Edward come?

EDWARD: Now Warwick, wilt thou humbly bend thy knee,
Call Edward king, and at his hands beg mercy,
And he shall pardon thee these outrages.

WARWICK: Nay rather, wilt thou draw thy forces hence,
Confess who set thee up and plucked thee down,
Call Warwick patron, and be penitent,
And thou shalt still remain the Duke of York.

RICHARD: I thought at least he would have said 'the King'.

WARWICK: 'Twas I that gave the kingdom to thy brother.
But weakling, Warwick takes his gift again;
And Henry is my king, Warwick his subject.

EDWARD: But Warwick's king is Edward's prisoner.

RICHARD: And ten to one you'll meet him in the Tower.
Come Warwick, take the time, kneel down, kneel down.

WARWICK: I had rather chop this hand off at a blow,
And with the other fling it at thy face,
Than bear so low a sail to strike to thee.
And lo, where George of Clarence stands by me,
With whom an upright zeal to right prevails
More than the nature of a brother's love.

EDWARD: A parley sound to George of Clarence!

*Sound a parley, and RICHARD and CLARENCE whisper
together; then RICHARD returns to EDWARD. CLARENCE
stands irresolute.*

WARWICK: Come Clarence come, thou wilt if Warwick call.

RICHARD: Come Clarence come, thou wilt if Edward call.

CLARENCE: Father of Warwick, know you what this means?

He takes his red rose out of his hat and throws it at WARWICK.

Look here, I throw my infamy at thee!
I will not ruinate my father's house,
Who gave his blood to lime the stones together,
And set up Lancaster. Why, trowest thou, Warwick,
That Clarence is so harsh, so blunt, unnatural,
To bend the fatal instruments of war
Against his brother and his lawful king?
Perhaps thou wilt object my holy oath:
To keep that oath were more impiety.
I am so sorry for my trespass made

That to deserve well at my brothers' hands,
I here proclaim myself thy mortal foe.
And so, proud-hearted Warwick, I defy thee,
And to my brothers turn my blushing cheeks.
Pardon me Edward, I will make amends.
And Richard, do not frown upon my faults,
For I will henceforth be no more unconstant.

EDWARD: Now welcome more, and ten times more beloved,
Than if thou never hadst deserved our hate.

RICHARD: Welcome, good Clarence, this is brother-like.

WARWICK: O passing traitor, perjured and unjust!
I bid thee battle, Edward, if thou dar'st.

EDWARD: Yes Warwick, Edward dares, and leads the way.
Lords, to the field – Saint George and victory!

*Alarums. Enter EDWARD bringing forth WARWICK,
wounded.*

So lie thou there. Die thou, and die our fear,
For Warwick was a bug that feared us all.

WARWICK: Ah, who is nigh? Come to me, friend or foe,
And tell me who is victor, York or Warwick?
Why ask I that? My mangled body shows
That I must yield my body to the earth.
These eyes, that now are dimmed with death's black veil,
Have been as piercing as the midday sun
To search the secret treasons of the world.
The wrinkles in my brows, now filled with blood,
Were likened oft to kingly sepulchres;
For who lived king, but I could dig his grave?
And who durst smile when Warwick bent his brow?
Lo now my glory smeared in dust and blood.
My parks, my walks, my manors that I had,
Even now forsake me, and of all my lands

Is nothing left me but my body's length.
Why, what is pomp, rule, reign, but earth and dust?
And live we how we can, yet die we must.

Enter EXETER and SOLDIERS.

EXETER: Ah, Warwick, Warwick, wert thou as we are,
We might recover all our loss again.
The Queen from France hath brought a puissant power.
Ah, couldst thou fly!

WARWICK: Fly, lords, and save yourselves,
For Warwick bids you all farewell, to meet in heaven.

He dies.

EXETER: Away, away, to meet the Queen's great power.

Here they bear away WARWICK's body. Exeunt.

Flourish. Enter EDWARD in triumph, with RICHARD, CLARENCE, and SOLDIERS.

EDWARD: Thus far our fortune keeps an upward course,
And we are graced with wreaths of victory.
But in the midst of this bright-shining day
I spy a black suspicious threatening cloud:
I mean, my lords, those powers that the Queen
Hath raised in Gallia have arrived our coast,
And as we hear, march on to fight with us.

RICHARD: The Queen is valued thirty thousand strong.
If she have time to breathe, be well assured,
Her faction will be full as strong as ours.

EDWARD: We are advertised by our loving friends
That they do hold their course toward Tewkesbury.
We'll thither straight, cry 'Courage!' and away.

Exeunt.

Scene 23

Tewkesbury.

Flourish. March. Enter MARGARET, PRINCE EDWARD, EXETER, and SOLDIERS.

MARGARET: Great lords, wise men ne'er sit and wail their
loss,
But cheerly seek how to redress their harms.
And though unskilful, why not Ned and I
For once allowed the skilful pilot's charge?
We will not from the helm to sit and weep,
But keep our course, though the rough wind say no,
From shelves and rocks that threaten us with wreck.
And what is Edward but a ruthless sea,
What Clarence but a quicksand of deceit,
And Richard but a ragged fatal rock?
All these the enemies to our poor barque.
Say you can swim – alas, 'tis but a while;
Tread on the sand – why, there you quickly sink;
Bestride the rock – the tide will wash you off,
Or else you famish: that's a threefold death.
This speak I, lords, to let you understand,
In case some one of you would fly from us,
That there's no hoped-for mercy with the brothers
More than with ruthless waves, with sands, and rocks.
Why, courage then: what cannot be avoided
'Twere childish weakness to lament or fear.

PRINCE EDWARD: Methinks a woman of this valiant spirit
Should, if a coward heard her speak these words,
Infuse his breast with magnanimity
And make him, naked, foil a man at arms.

Enter a MESSENGER.

MESSENGER: Prepare you, lords, for Edward is at hand.

EXETER: I thought no less. It is his policy
  To haste thus fast to find us unprovided.

PRINCE EDWARD: But he's deceived, we are in readiness.

MARGARET: Lords, knights, and gentlemen, Henry your King
  Is prisoner to the foe, his state usurped,
  His realm a slaughter-house, his subjects slain,
  His statutes cancelled, and his treasure spent;
  And yonder is the wolf that makes this spoil.
  You fight in justice; then in God's name, lords,
  Be valiant, and give signal to the fight.

  *Flourish and march. Enter EDWARD, RICHARD and
  CLARENCE, with SOLDIERS.*

EDWARD: Brave followers, yonder stands the thorny wood
  Which by the heavens' assistance and your strength,
  Must by the roots be hewn up yet ere night.
  I need not add more fuel to your fire,
  For well I wot ye blaze to burn them out.
  Give signal to the fight, and to it, lords.

  Alarum, retreat, excursions.

  *Flourish. Enter EDWARD, RICHARD, CLARENCE, with
  MARGARET and PRINCE EDWARD, guarded.*

  Now here a period of tumultuous broils.
  Edward, what satisfaction canst thou make
  For bearing arms, for stirring up my subjects,
  And all the trouble thou hast turned me to?

PRINCE EDWARD: Speak like a subject, proud ambitious
                                      York.

  Suppose that I am now my father's mouth –
  Resign thy chair, and where I stand, kneel thou,
  Whilst I propose the self-same words to thee,
  Which, traitor, thou wouldst have me answer to.

MARGARET: Ah that thy father had been so resolved.

RICHARD: That you might still have worn the petticoat
    And ne'er have stolen the breech from Lancaster.

PRINCE EDWARD: Let Aesop fable in a winter's night –
    His currish riddles sorts not with this place.

RICHARD: By heaven, brat, I'll plague ye for that word.

MARGARET: Ay, thou wast born to be a plague to men.

RICHARD: For God's sake take away this captive scold.

PRINCE EDWARD: Nay, take away this scolding
                                        crookback rather.

EDWARD: Peace, wilful boy, or I will charm your tongue.

CLARENCE: Untutored lad, thou art too malapert.

PRINCE EDWARD: I know my duty, you are all undutiful.
    Lascivious Edward, and thou, perjured George,
    And thou, misshapen Dick – I tell ye all
    I am your better, traitors as ye are,
    And thou usurp'st my father's right and mine.

EDWARD: Take that, the likeness of this railer here.
                                        (*Stabs him.*)

RICHARD: Sprawl'st thou? Take that, to end thy agony.
                                        (*Stabs him.*)

CLARENCE: And there's for twitting me with perjury.
                                        (*Stabs him.*)

MARGARET: O kill me too!

RICHARD: Marry, and shall.

He offers to kill her.

EDWARD: Hold, Richard, hold, for we have done too much.

RICHARD: Why should she live to fill the world with words?

EDWARD: What, doth she swoon? Use means for her recovery.

RICHARD: Clarence, excuse me to the King my brother.
    I'll hence to London on a serious matter.
    Ere ye come there, be sure to hear some news.

CLARENCE: What? What?

RICHARD: The Tower, the Tower. (*Exit.*)

MARGARET: O Ned, sweet Ned, speak to thy mother, boy.
    Butchers and villains, bloody cannibals,
    How sweet a plant have you untimely cropped!
    You have no children, butchers; if you had,
    The thought of them would have stirred up remorse.
    But if you ever chance to have a child,
    Look in his youth to have him so cut off
    As, deathsmen, you have rid this sweet young Prince!

EDWARD: Away with her, go bear her hence perforce.

MARGARET: Nay, never bear me hence, dispatch me here.
    Here sheathe thy sword, I'll pardon thee my death.
    What, wilt thou not? Then Clarence, do it thou.

CLARENCE: By heaven, I will not do thee so much ease.

MARGARET: Good Clarence, do; sweet Clarence, do thou
                                    do it.

CLARENCE: Didst thou not hear me swear I would not do it?

MARGARET: Ay, but thou usest to forswear thyself.
    'Twas sin before, but now 'tis charity.
    What, wilt thou not? Where is that devil's butcher,
    Hard-favoured Richard? Richard, where art thou?

EDWARD: Away, I say – I charge ye, bear her hence.

MARGARET: So come to you and yours as to this Prince!
                                  (*Exit, guarded.*)

EDWARD: Where's Richard gone?

CLARENCE: To London all in post, and as I guess,
    To make a bloody supper in the Tower.

EDWARD: He's sudden if a thing comes in his head.
    Now march we hence. Discharge the common sort
    With pay and thanks, and let's away to London,
    And see our gentle Queen how well she fares.
    By this I hope she hath a son for me.

Exeunt.

Scene 24

The Tower.

Enter RICHARD to KING HENRY.

RICHARD: Good day, my lord, what at your book so hard?

KING HENRY: Ay, my good lord – 'my lord', I should say
                                          rather.
    'Tis sin to flatter; 'good' was little better.
    'Good Gloucester' and 'good devil' were alike.
    But wherefore dost thou come? Is't for my life?

RICHARD: Think'st thou I am an executioner?

KING HENRY: A persecutor I am sure thou art;
    If murdering innocents be executing,
    Why then thou art an executioner.

RICHARD: Thy son I killed for his presumption.

KING HENRY: Hadst thou been killed when first thou
                           didst presume,
    Thou hadst not lived to kill a son of mine.
    And thus I prophesy: that many a thousand
    Which now mistrust no parcel of my fear,
    And many an old man's sigh, and many a widow's,
    And many an orphan's water-standing eye –
    Men for their sons', wives for their husbands',

Orphans for their parents' timeless death –
Shall rue the hour that ever thou wast born.
Thy mother felt more than a mother's pain,
And yet brought forth less than a mother's hope,
To wit, an indigested and deformèd lump,
Not like the fruit of such a goodly tree.
Teeth hadst thou in thy head when thou wast born,
To signify thou cam'st to bite the world;
And if the rest be true which I have heard
Thou cam'st –

RICHARD: I'll hear no more. Die, prophet, in thy speech,

He stabs him.

For this, amongst the rest, was I ordained.

KING HENRY: Ay, and for much more slaughter after this.
O God forgive my sins, and pardon thee.

He dies.

RICHARD: What, will the aspiring blood of Lancaster
Sink in the ground? I thought it would have mounted.
If any spark of life be yet remaining,
Down, down to hell, and say I sent thee thither.

He stabs him again.

I that have neither pity, love, nor fear.
Indeed, 'tis true that Henry told me of,
For I have often heard my mother say
I came into the world with my legs forward.
Had I not reason, think ye, to make haste,
And seek their ruin that usurped our right?
The midwife wondered and the women cried
'O Jesus bless us, he is born with teeth!'
And so I was, which plainly signified
That I should snarl and bite and play the dog.
Then since the heavens have shaped my body so,
Let hell make crook'd my mind to answer it.

I had no father, I am like no father;
I have no brother, I am like no brother;
And this word 'love' which greybeards call divine,
Be resident in men like one another
And not in me; I am myself alone.
King Henry and the prince his son are gone;
Clarence, thy turn is next, and then the rest,
Counting myself but bad till I be best.
I'll throw thy body in another room
And triumph, Henry, in thy day of doom.

Exit with the body.

Scene 25

The Royal Palace.

Flourish. Enter KING EDWARD, Queen Elizabeth (LADY GREY), CLARENCE, RICHARD, and ATTENDANTS.

EDWARD: Once more we sit in England's royal throne,
　　　Repurchased with the blood of enemies.
　　　Come hither, Bess, and let me kiss my boy.
　　　Young Ned, for thee, thine uncles and myself
　　　Have in our armours watched the winter's night,
　　　Went all afoot in summer's scalding heat,
　　　That thou mightst repossess the crown in peace;
　　　And of our labours thou shalt reap the gain.

RICHARD: *(Aside.)* I'll blast his harvest, ere his corn be ripe.

EDWARD: Clarence and Gloucester, love my lovely queen;
　　　And kiss your princely nephew, brothers both.

CLARENCE: The duty that I owe unto your majesty
　　　I seal upon the lips of this sweet babe.

LADY GREY: Thanks noble Clarence, worthy brother,
　　　　　　　　　　　　　　　　　　　　thanks.

RICHARD: And that I love the tree from whence thou
sprang'st,

    Witness the loving kiss I give the fruit.
    (*Aside.*) To say the truth, so Judas kissed his master,
    And cried 'All hail!' whenas he meant all harm.

EDWARD: Now am I seated as my soul delights,
    Having my country's peace and brothers' loves.

CLARENCE: What will your grace have done with Margaret?

EDWARD: Away with her, and waft her hence to France.
    And now what rests but that we spend the time
    With stately triumphs, mirthful comic shows,
    Such as befits the pleasure of the court?
    Sound drums and trumpets, farewell sour annoy!
    For here I hope begins our lasting joy.

    Flourish. Exeunt.